HOW TO DRAW

Cute and Magical Pictures Like the Pros

Table of Contents

THE WEAVER DOODLE DIFFERENCE

Discover what makes Weaver Doodle unique by visiting our Author Profile page.

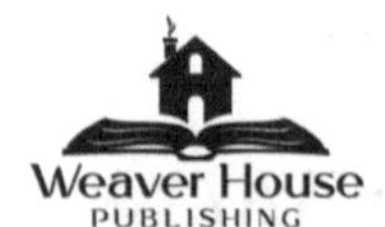

Weaver House Publishing LLC

SUPPLIES

Gather Supplies

Here's what you'll need:
- Grab your favorite pencil and an eraser
- Keep a pencil sharpener close by
- A ruler is a great tool to draw grids

TIPS

Helpful tips

- Go slow. Take your time and draw each square as accurate as you can get it.
- It's okay to make mistakes—that's what erasers are for. Draw with a light touch until you're certain you want to keep that line. You'll get better with practice.
- Stay with one square until its completed. Pay attention to the small details. You'll be sketching like a pro in no time.
- The complexity of the images in this book are geared toward the brand-new pencil sketch artist. Some images are more elaborate than others and require more "sketch focus". Start with the less-complicated images first then graduate yourself up as your skill increases.
- If you want to add some flare, fill in the completed image with colored pencils.
- When you're ready to take your pencil artistry to the next level, consider investing in a set of drawing pencils. A wide range of pencil grades will allow you to draw smaller lines and add darker shades.
- Practice, practice, practice. The more you train, the faster your sketching skills will advance.

Turn the page to begin sketching like the pros!

Drawing with pencil is fun and easy!

HOW TO USE THIS BOOK

Sketch the Picture

1. Use the picture on the top left as a GUIDE to refer back to as you sketch.
2. One square at a time, TRACE the warmup picture to get your drawing hand ready for action.
3. One square at a time, fill in the missing squares on the LEFT side.
4. One square at a time, fill in the missing squares on the RIGHT side.
5. One square at a time, draw the ENTIRE PICTURE.
6. You're on your own now. Draw the grid yourself then sketch one square at a time.

Erase the grid and touch up any flaws.

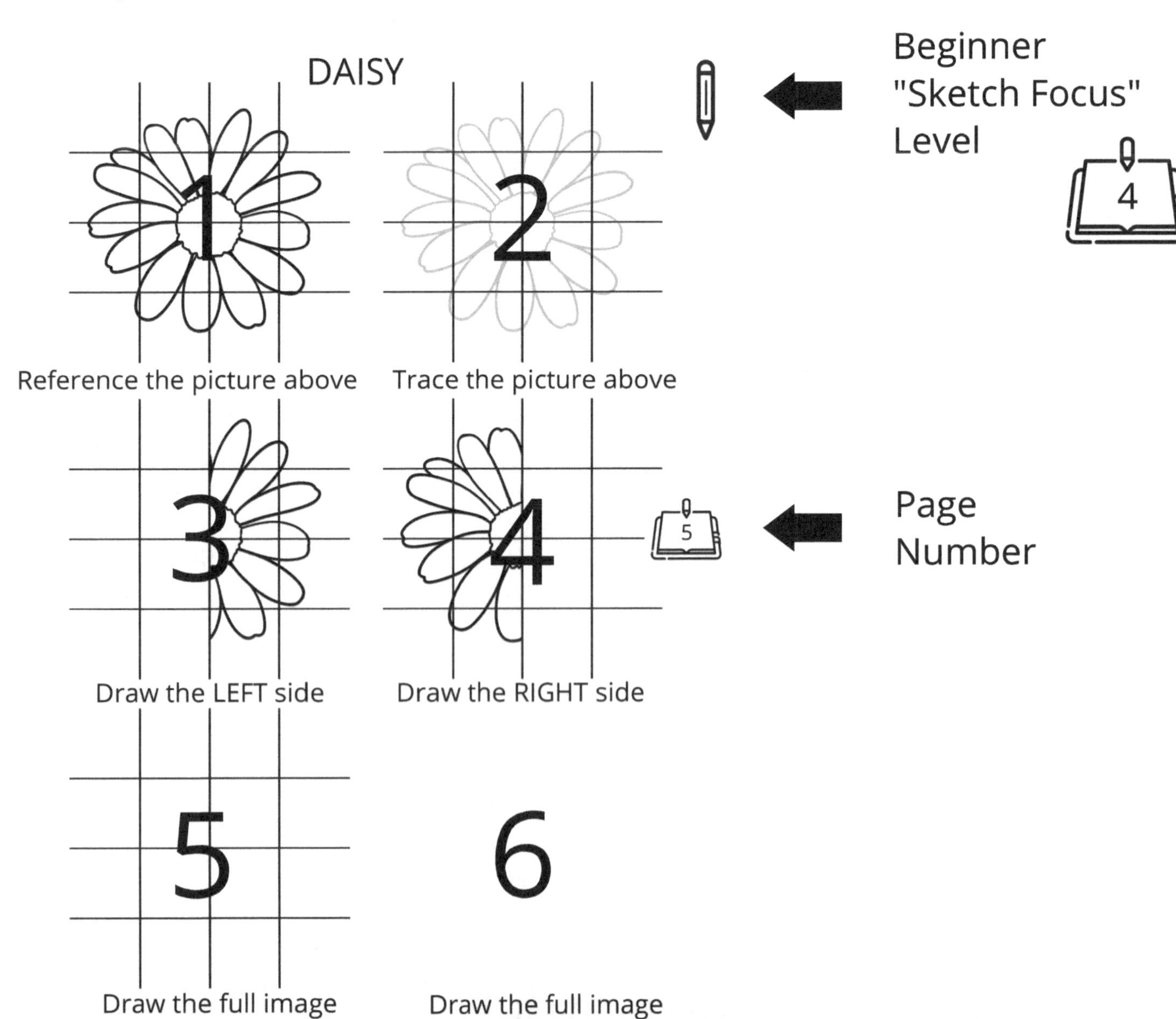

DAISY

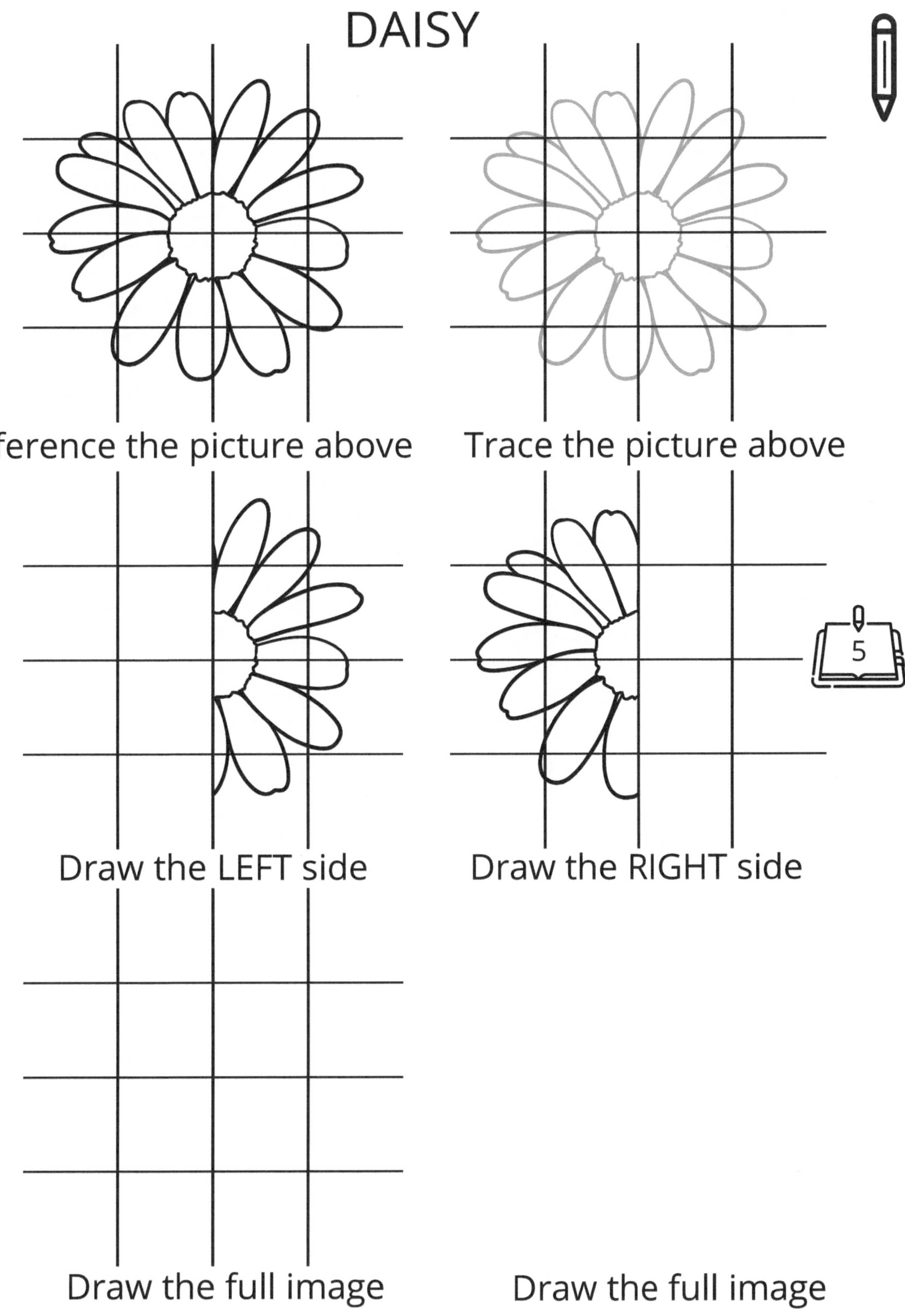

Reference the picture above
Trace the picture above
Draw the LEFT side
Draw the RIGHT side
Draw the full image
Draw the full image

TULIP

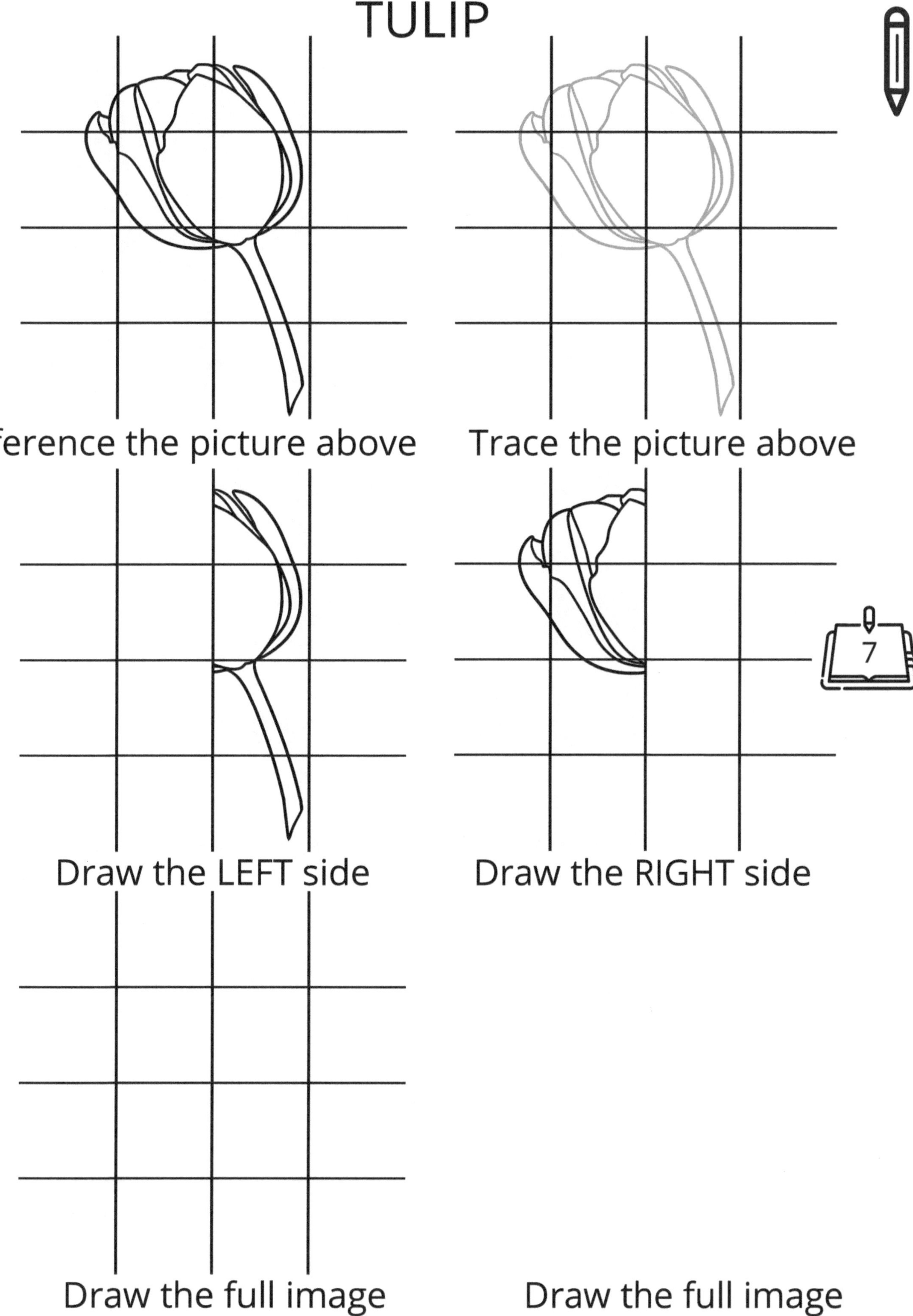

Reference the picture above
Trace the picture above
Draw the LEFT side
Draw the RIGHT side
7
Draw the full image
Draw the full image

ROSE

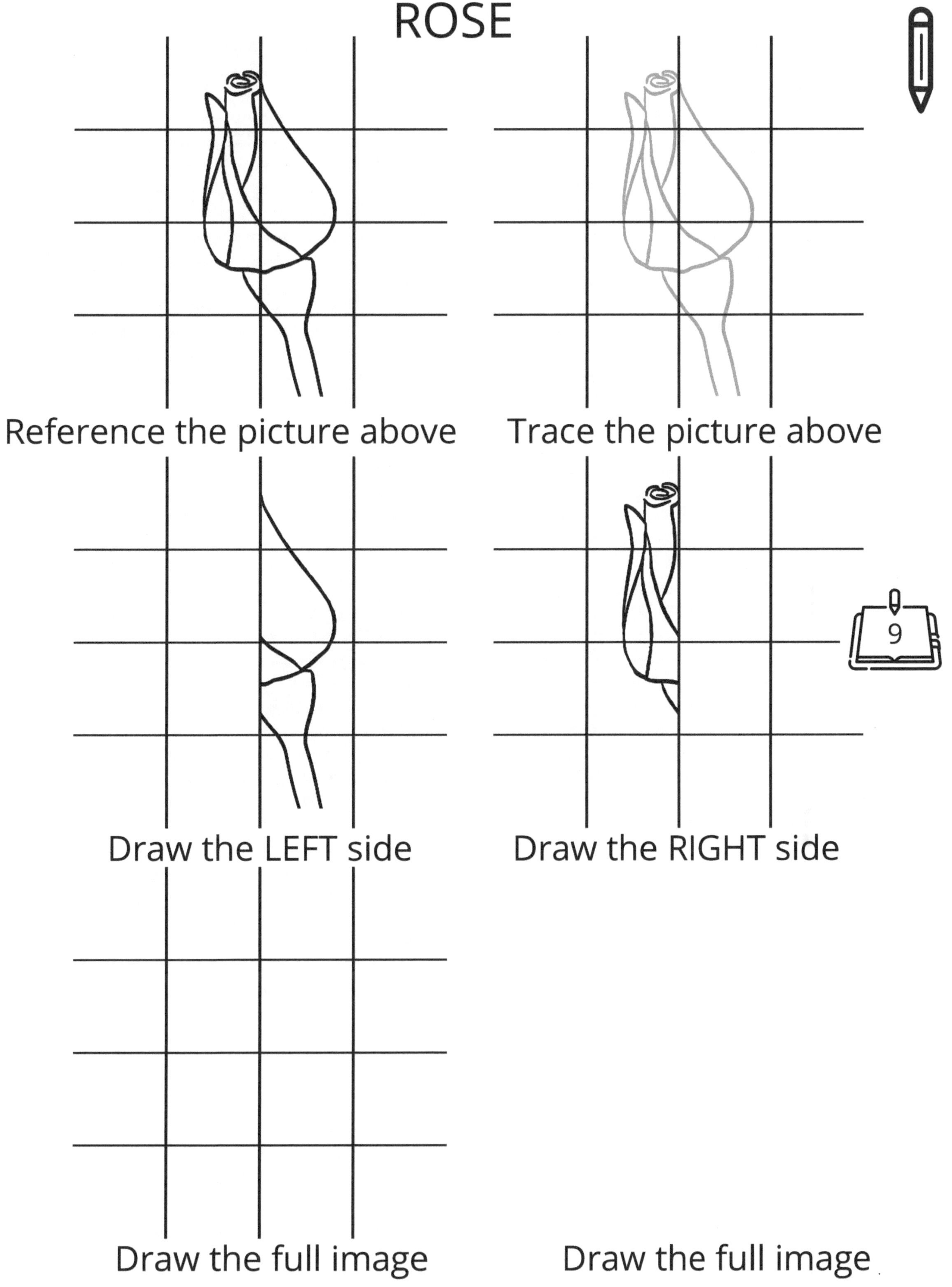
Reference the picture above
Trace the picture above
Draw the LEFT side
Draw the RIGHT side
Draw the full image
Draw the full image

SUNFLOWER

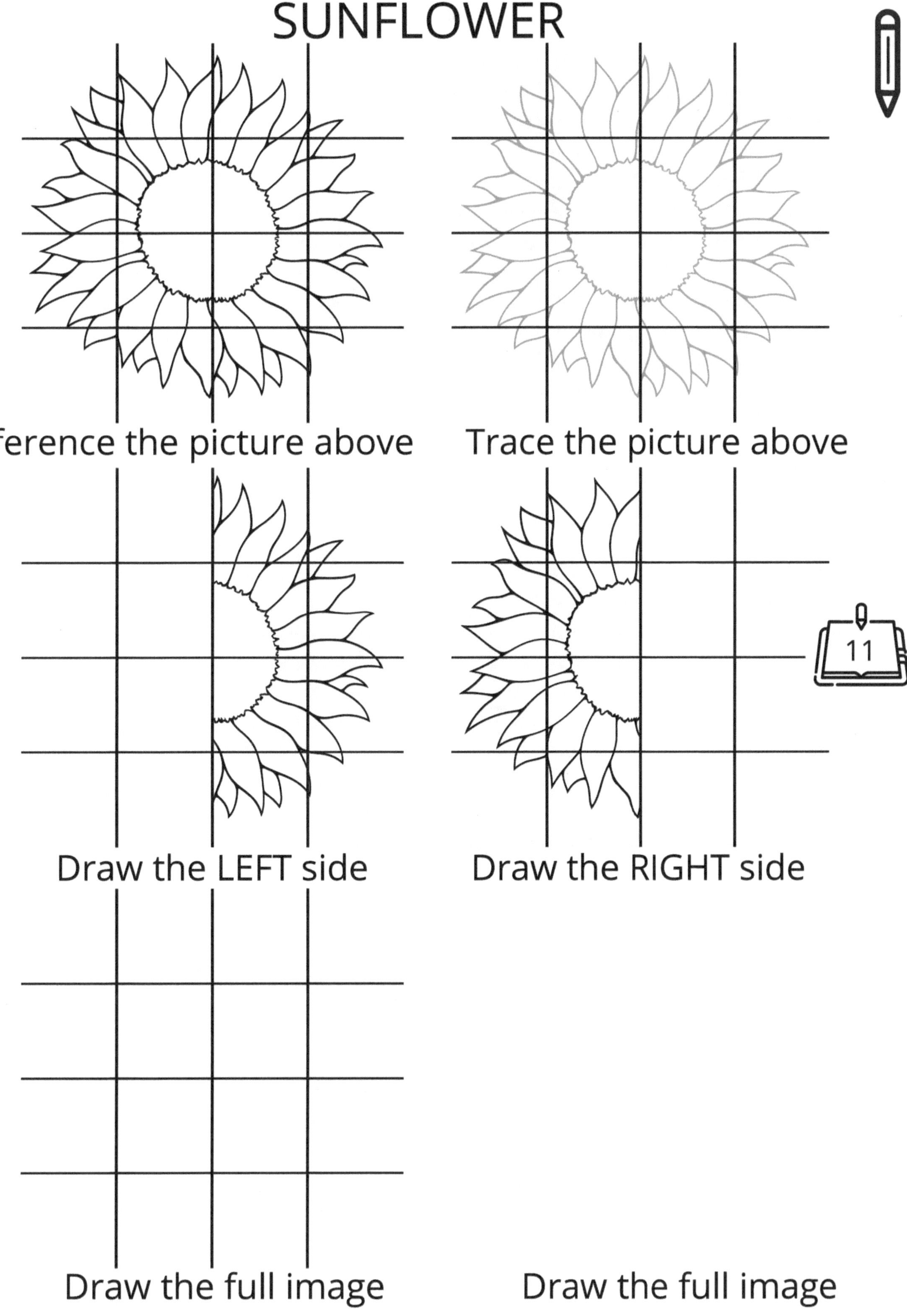
Reference the picture above
Trace the picture above
Draw the LEFT side
Draw the RIGHT side
Draw the full image
Draw the full image

MORNING GLORY

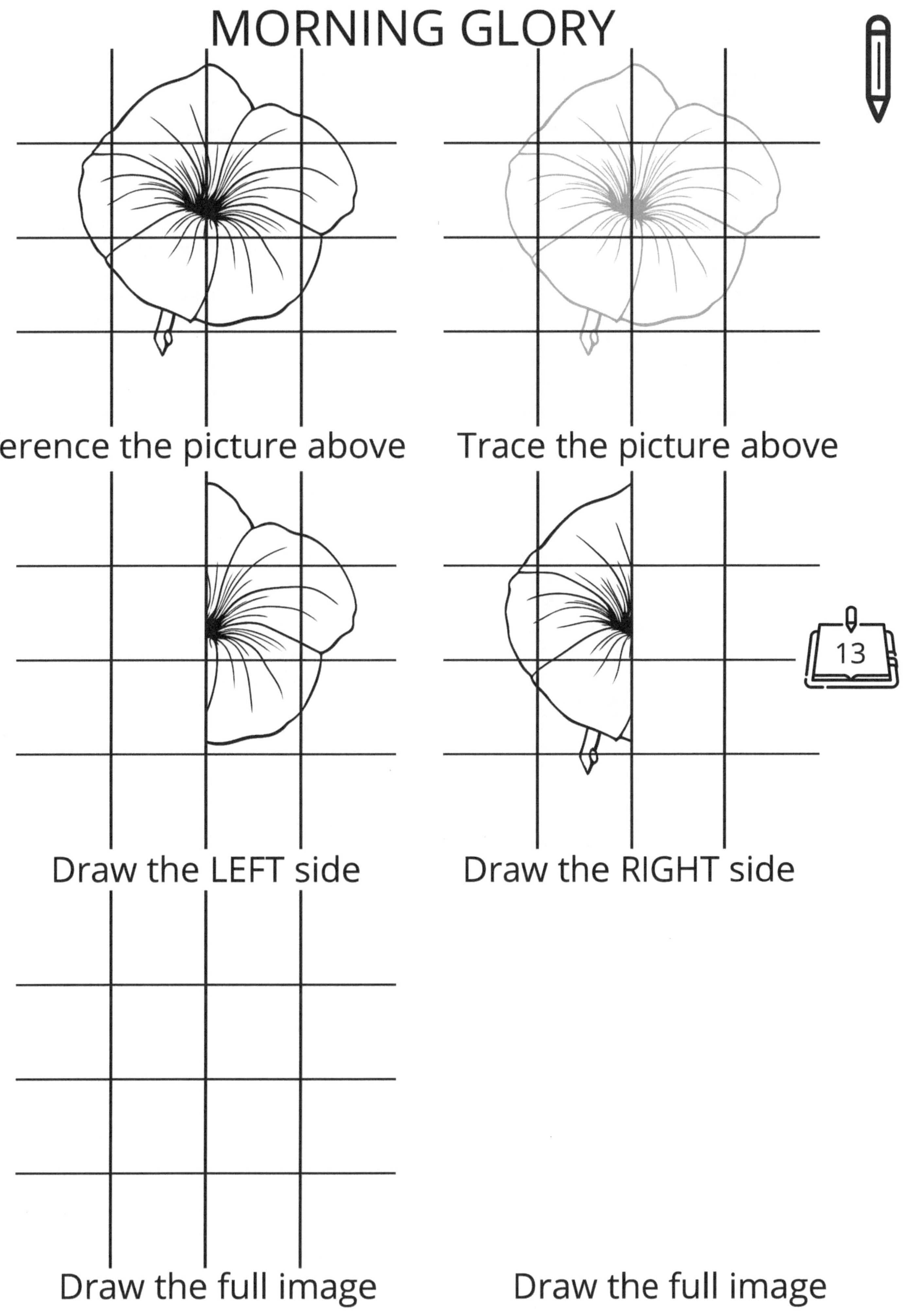

RAINBOW

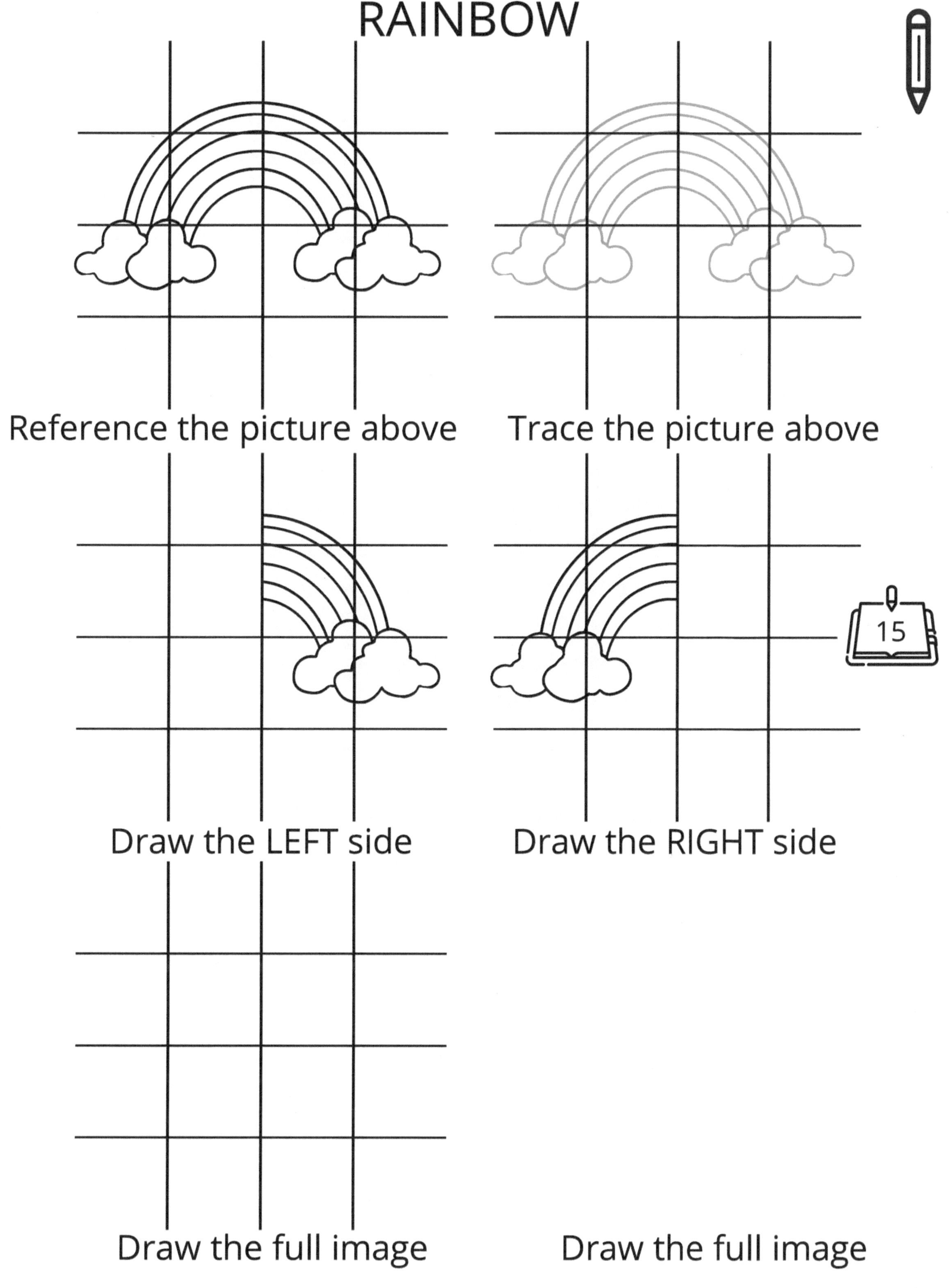
Reference the picture above
Trace the picture above
Draw the LEFT side
Draw the RIGHT side
15
Draw the full image
Draw the full image

SATURN

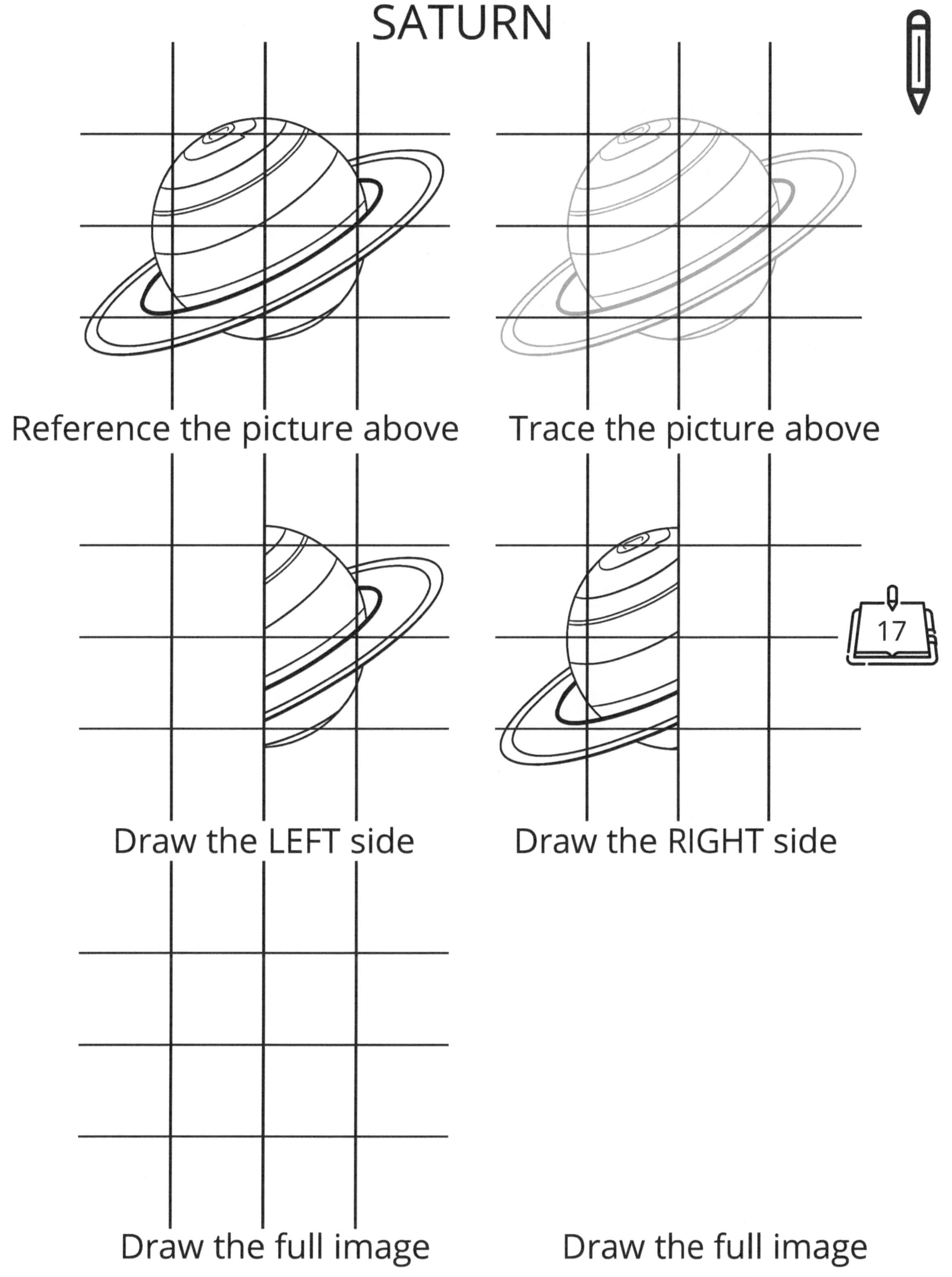

Reference the picture above
Trace the picture above
Draw the LEFT side
Draw the RIGHT side
17
Draw the full image
Draw the full image

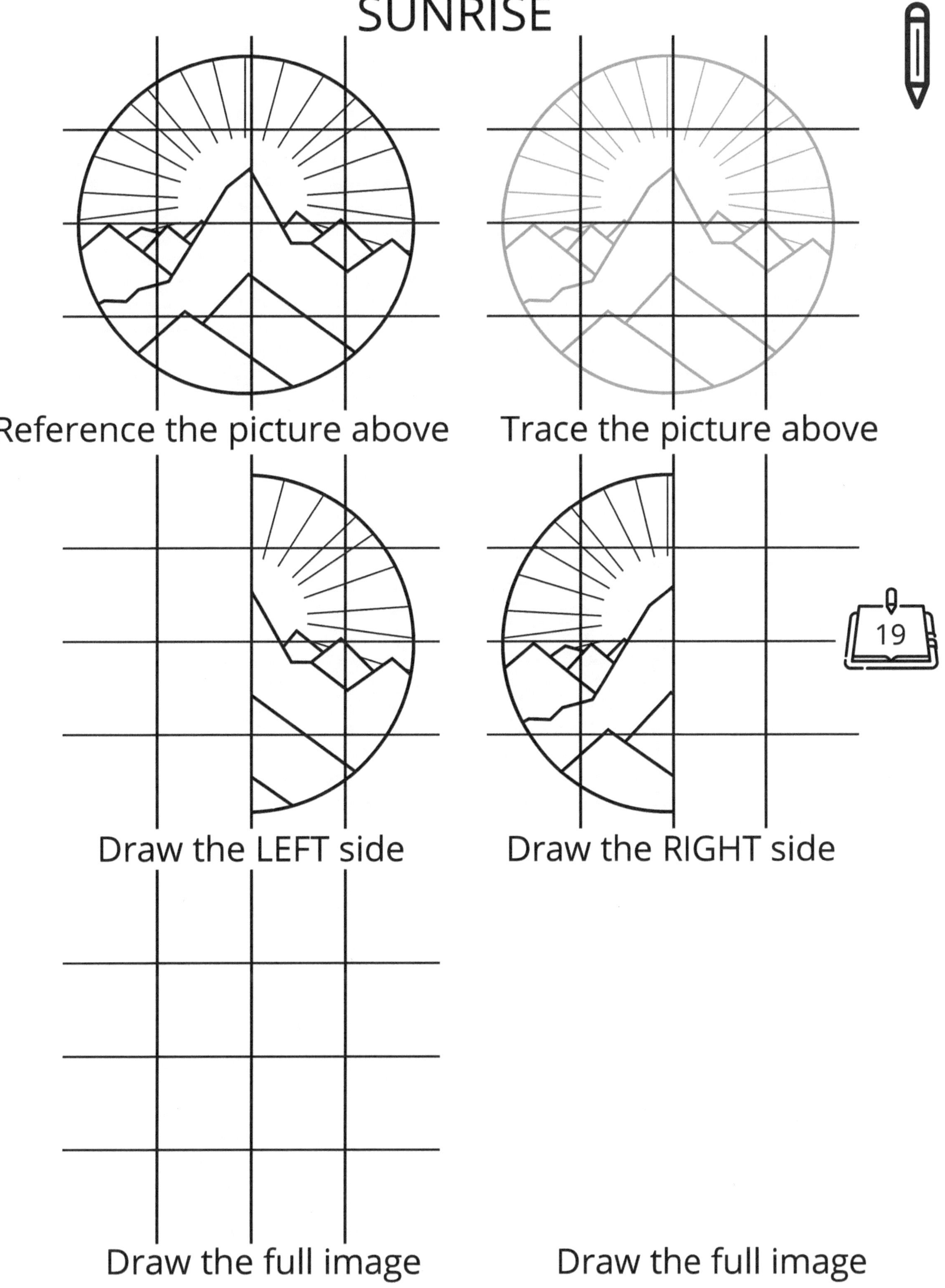
SUNRISE
Reference the picture above
Trace the picture above
Draw the LEFT side
Draw the RIGHT side
19
Draw the full image
Draw the full image

MUSHROOM

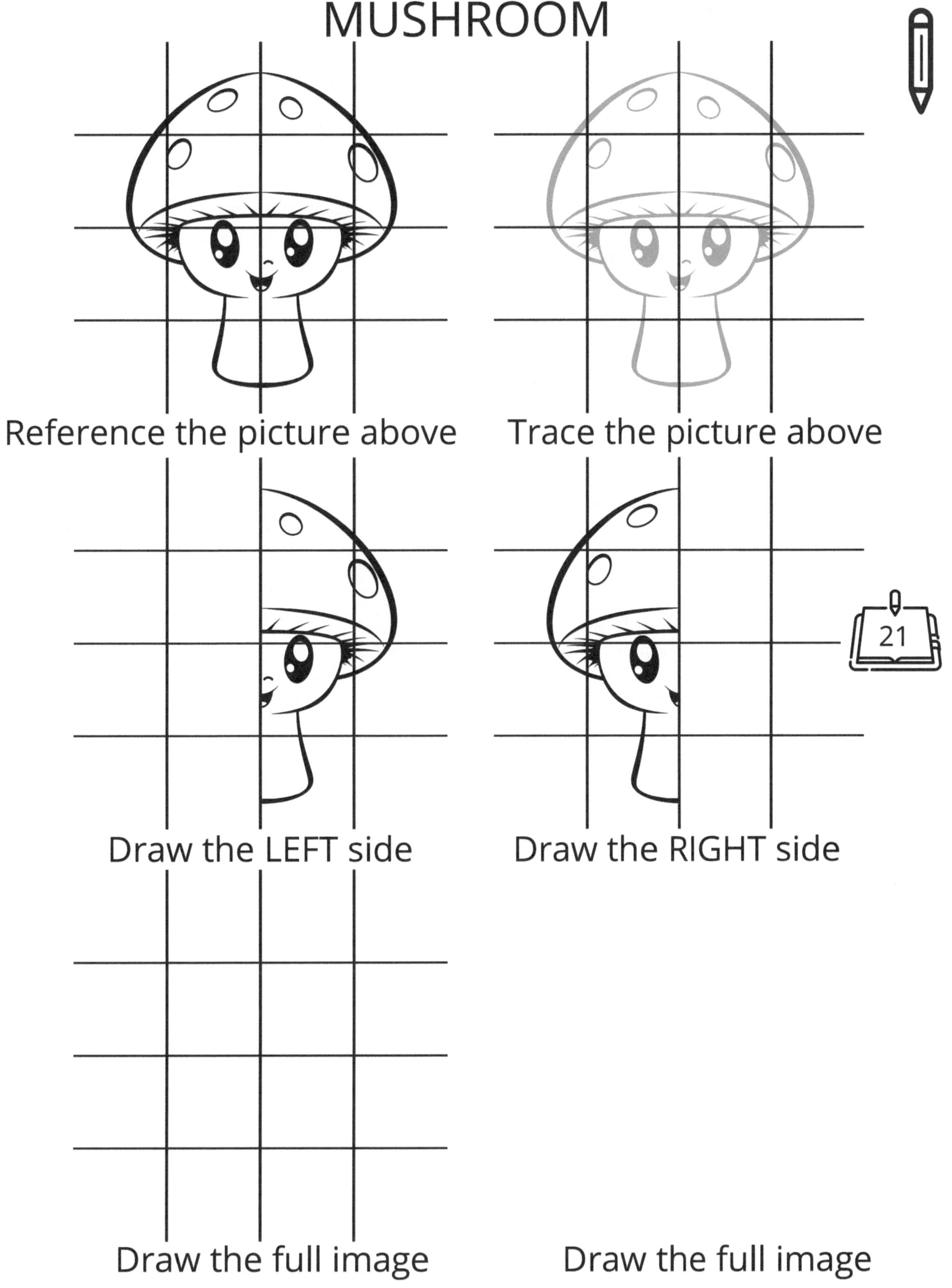
Reference the picture above
Trace the picture above
Draw the LEFT side
Draw the RIGHT side
Draw the full image
Draw the full image

BIG DIPPER

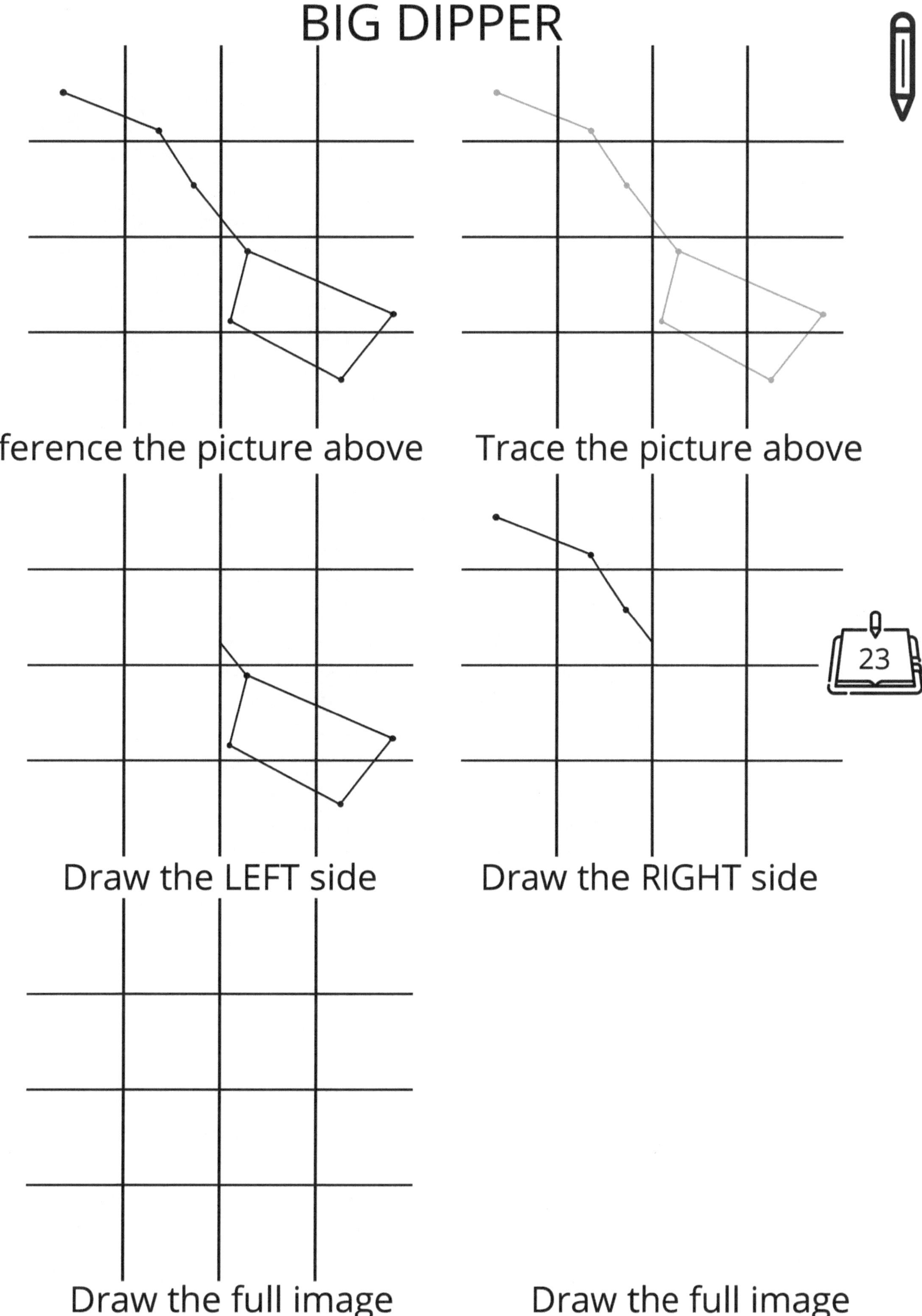

Reference the picture above
Trace the picture above
Draw the LEFT side
Draw the RIGHT side
23
Draw the full image
Draw the full image

CUPCAKE

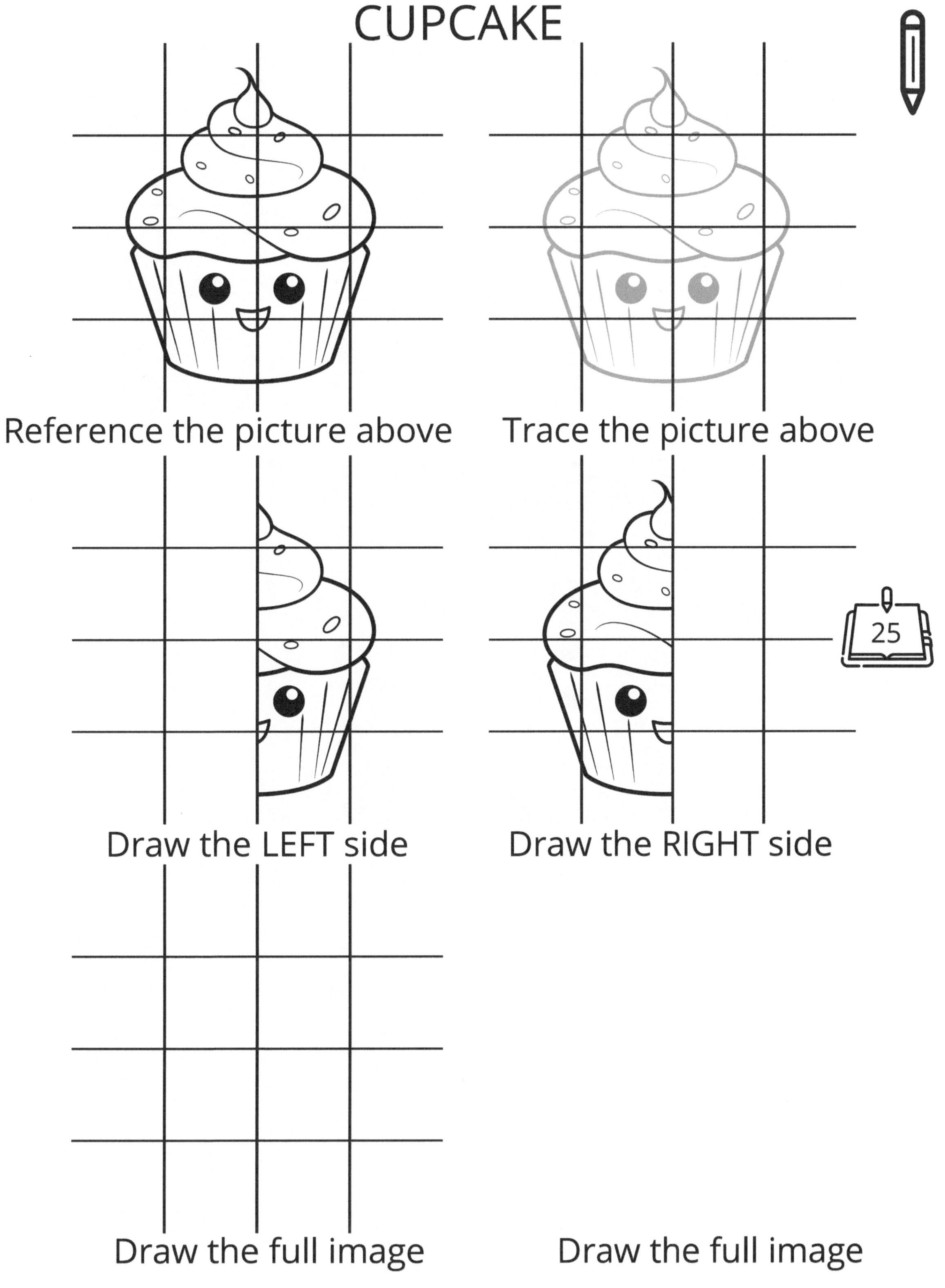

Reference the picture above
Trace the picture above
Draw the LEFT side
Draw the RIGHT side
Draw the full image
Draw the full image

ICE CREAM CONE

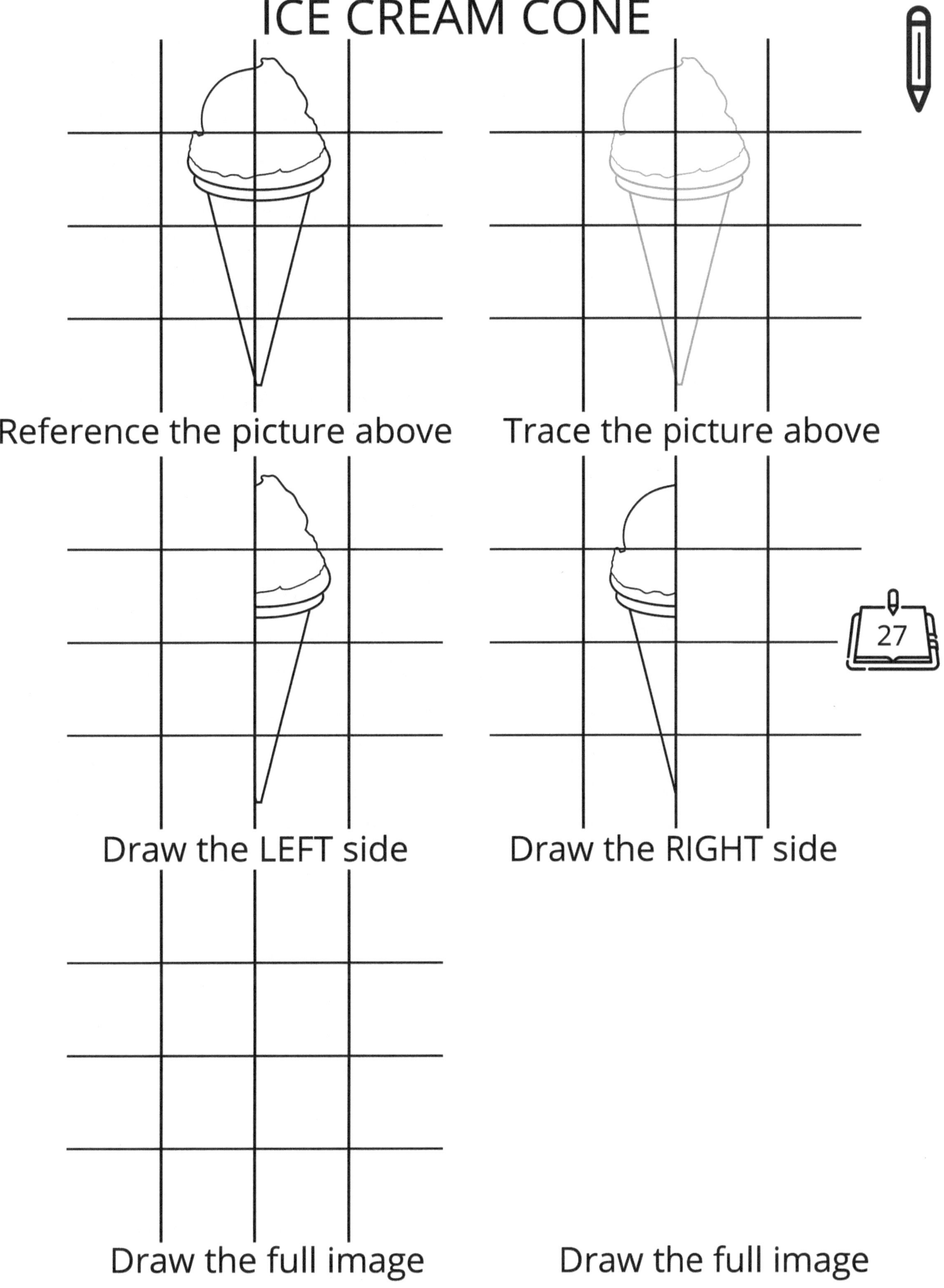

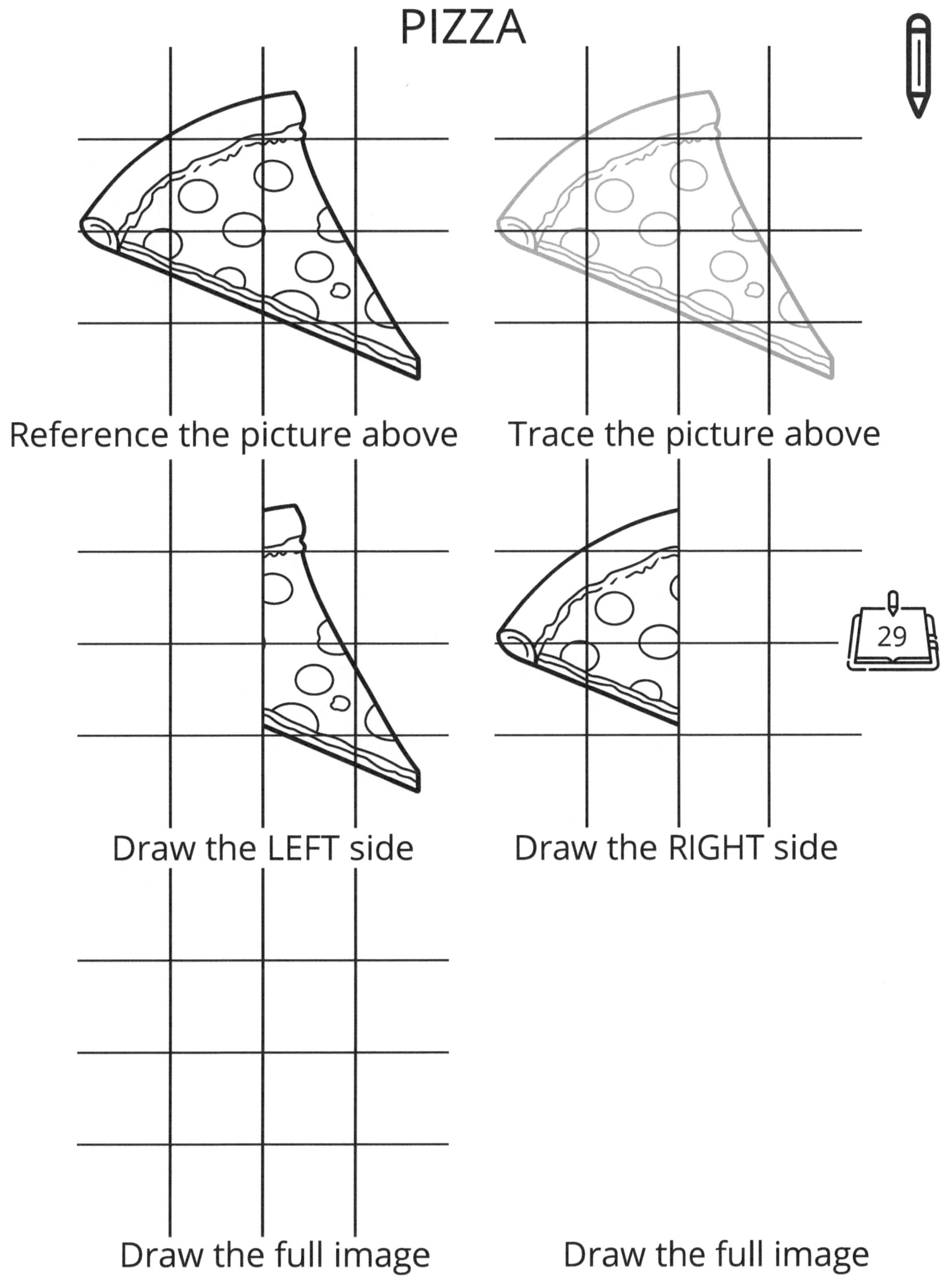
PIZZA
Reference the picture above
Trace the picture above
Draw the LEFT side
Draw the RIGHT side
29
Draw the full image
Draw the full image

WATERMELON

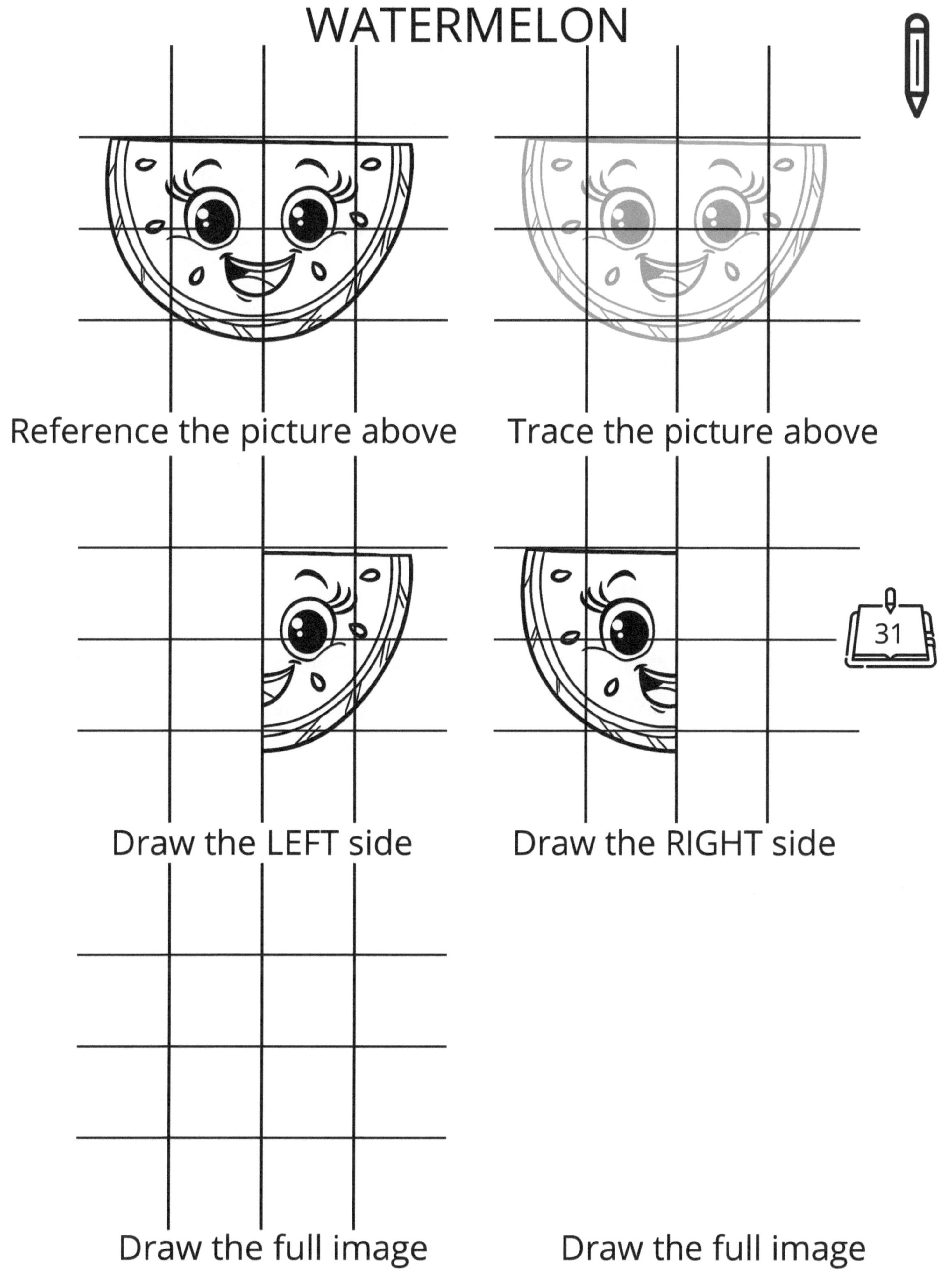

Reference the picture above
Trace the picture above
Draw the LEFT side
Draw the RIGHT side
Draw the full image
Draw the full image

STRAWBERRY

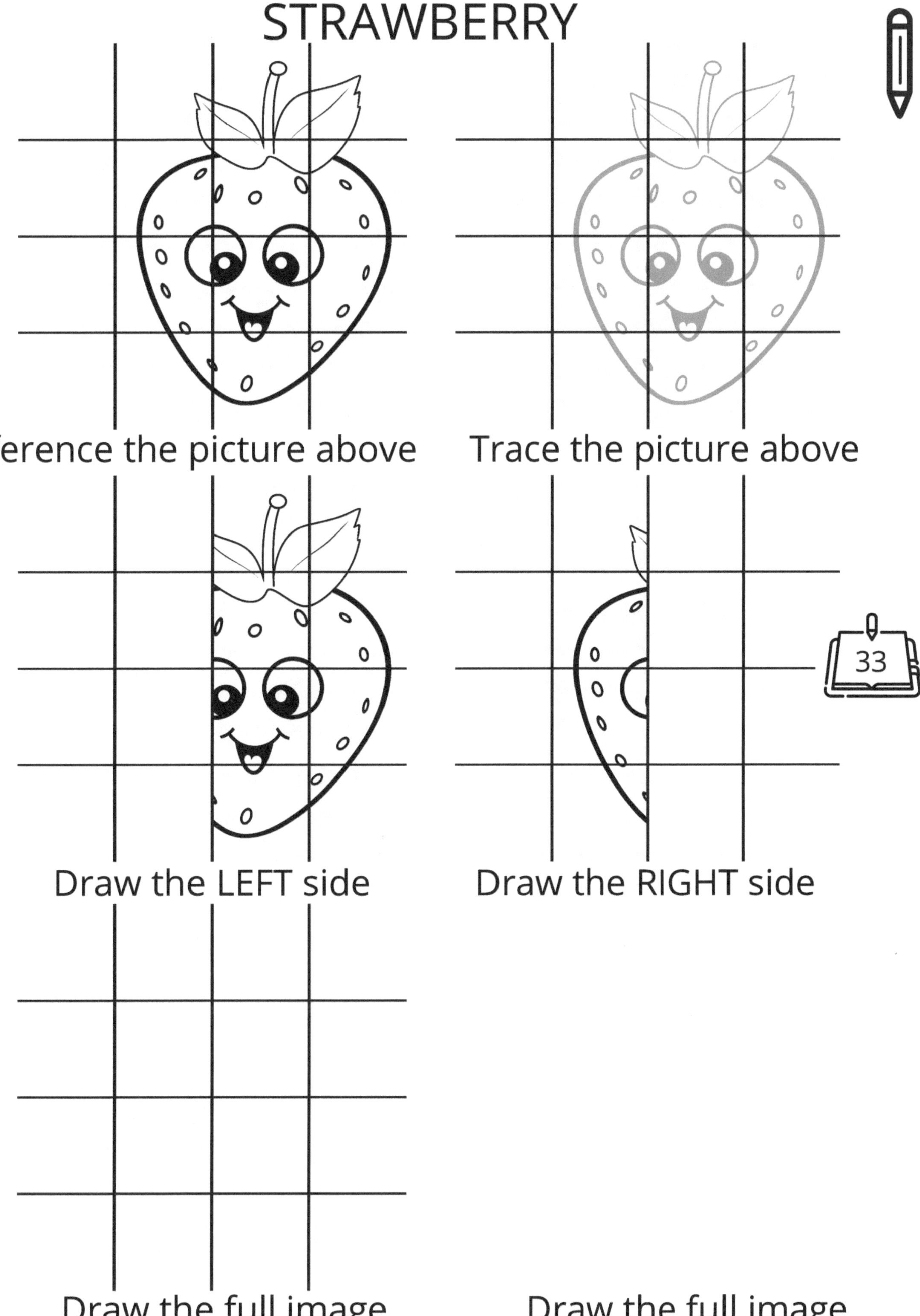
Reference the picture above
Trace the picture above
Draw the LEFT side
Draw the RIGHT side
Draw the full image
Draw the full image

QUEEN

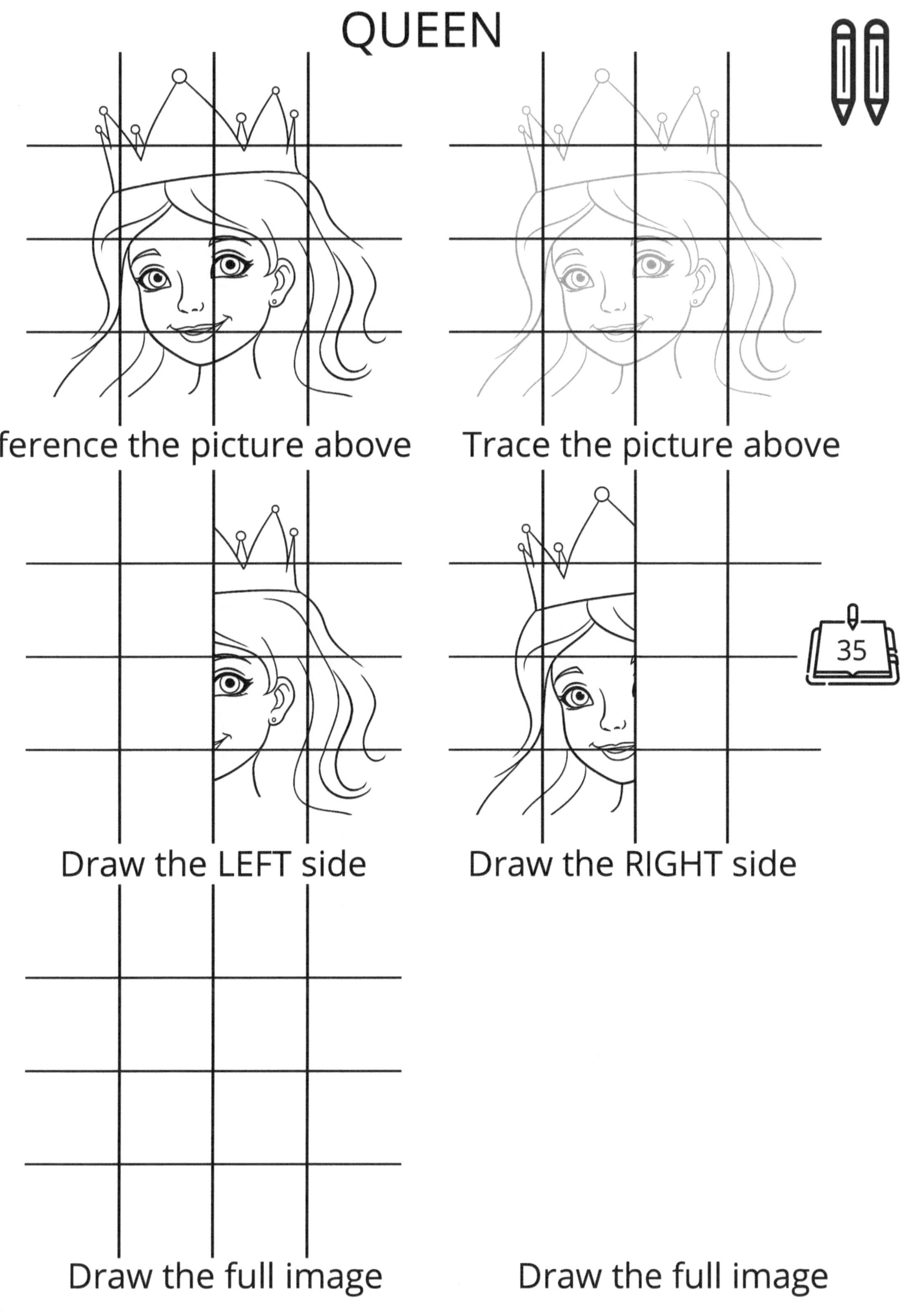
Reference the picture above
Trace the picture above
Draw the LEFT side
Draw the RIGHT side
Draw the full image
Draw the full image

WITCH

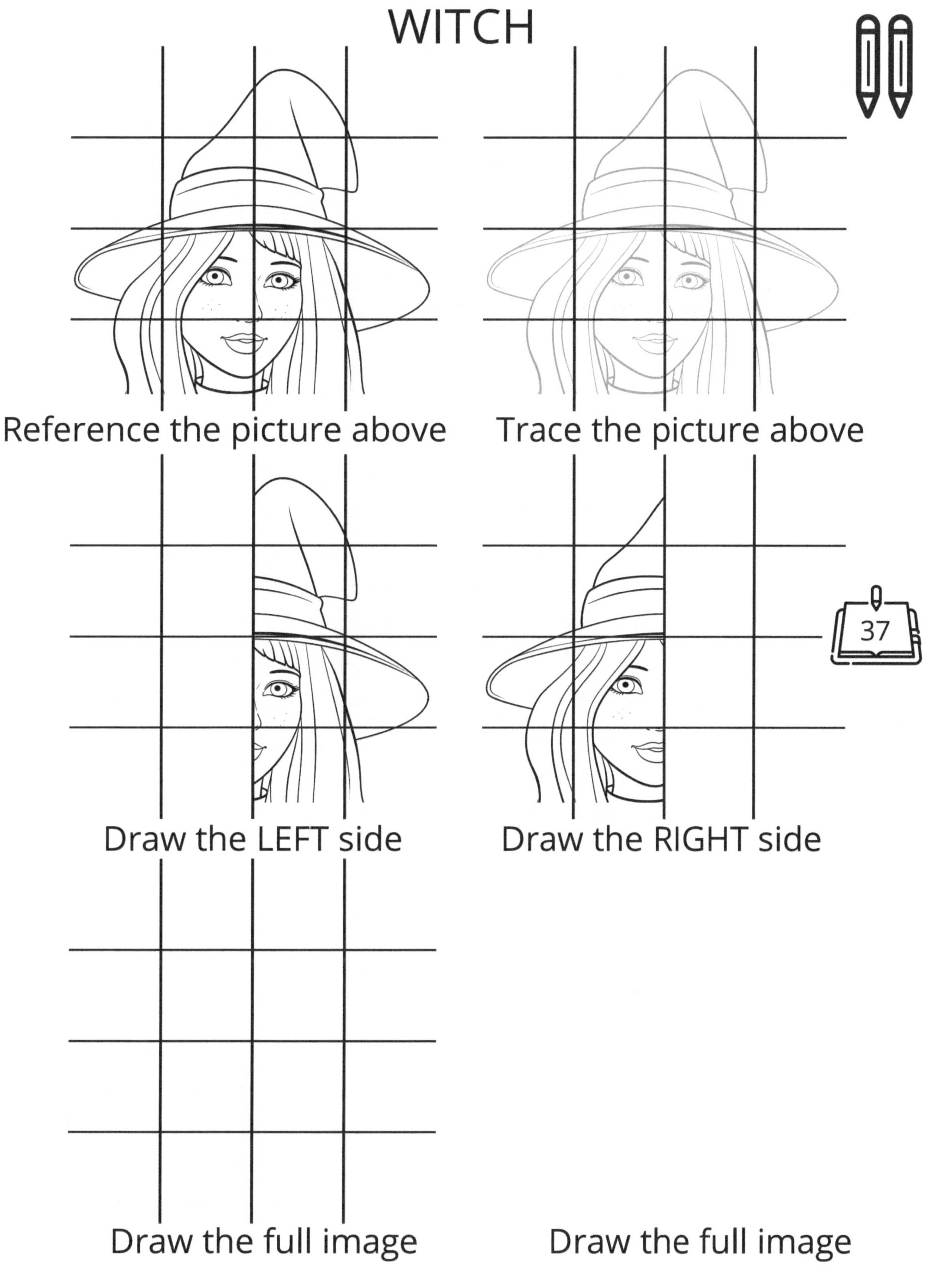

Reference the picture above
Trace the picture above
Draw the LEFT side
Draw the RIGHT side
37
Draw the full image
Draw the full image

WIZARD

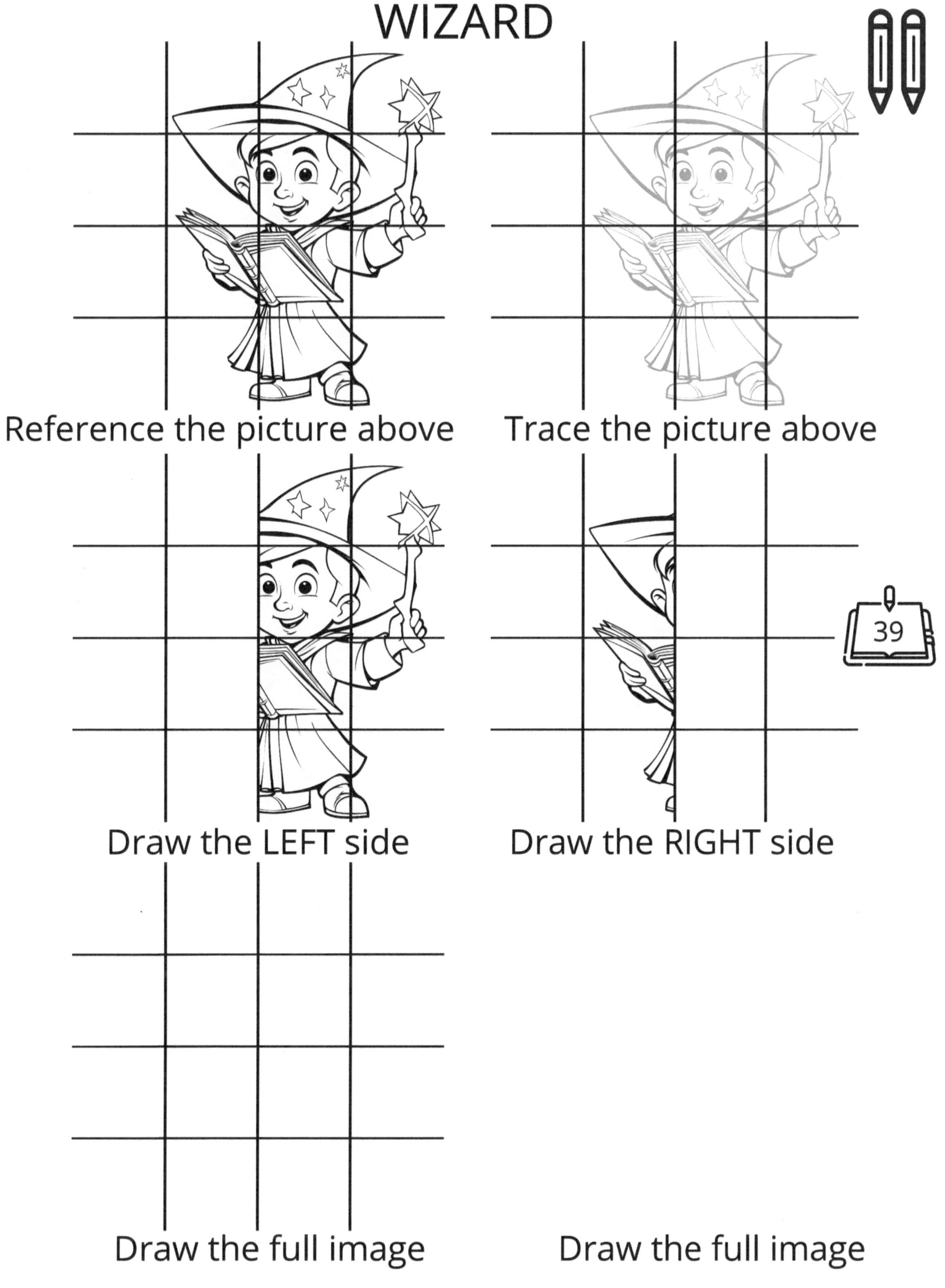
Reference the picture above
Trace the picture above
Draw the LEFT side
Draw the RIGHT side
Draw the full image
Draw the full image

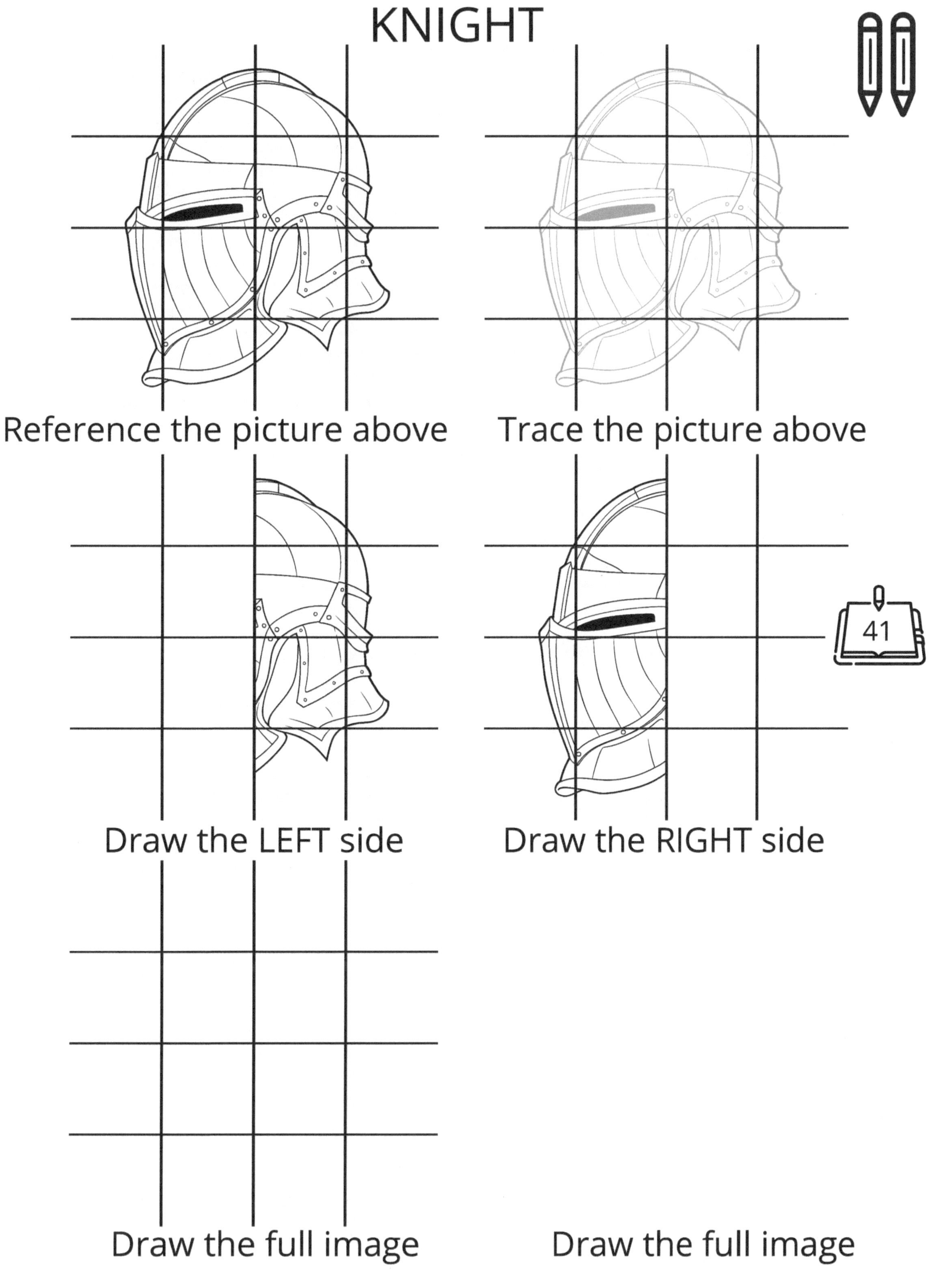
KNIGHT
Reference the picture above
Trace the picture above
Draw the LEFT side
Draw the RIGHT side
41
Draw the full image
Draw the full image

JESTER

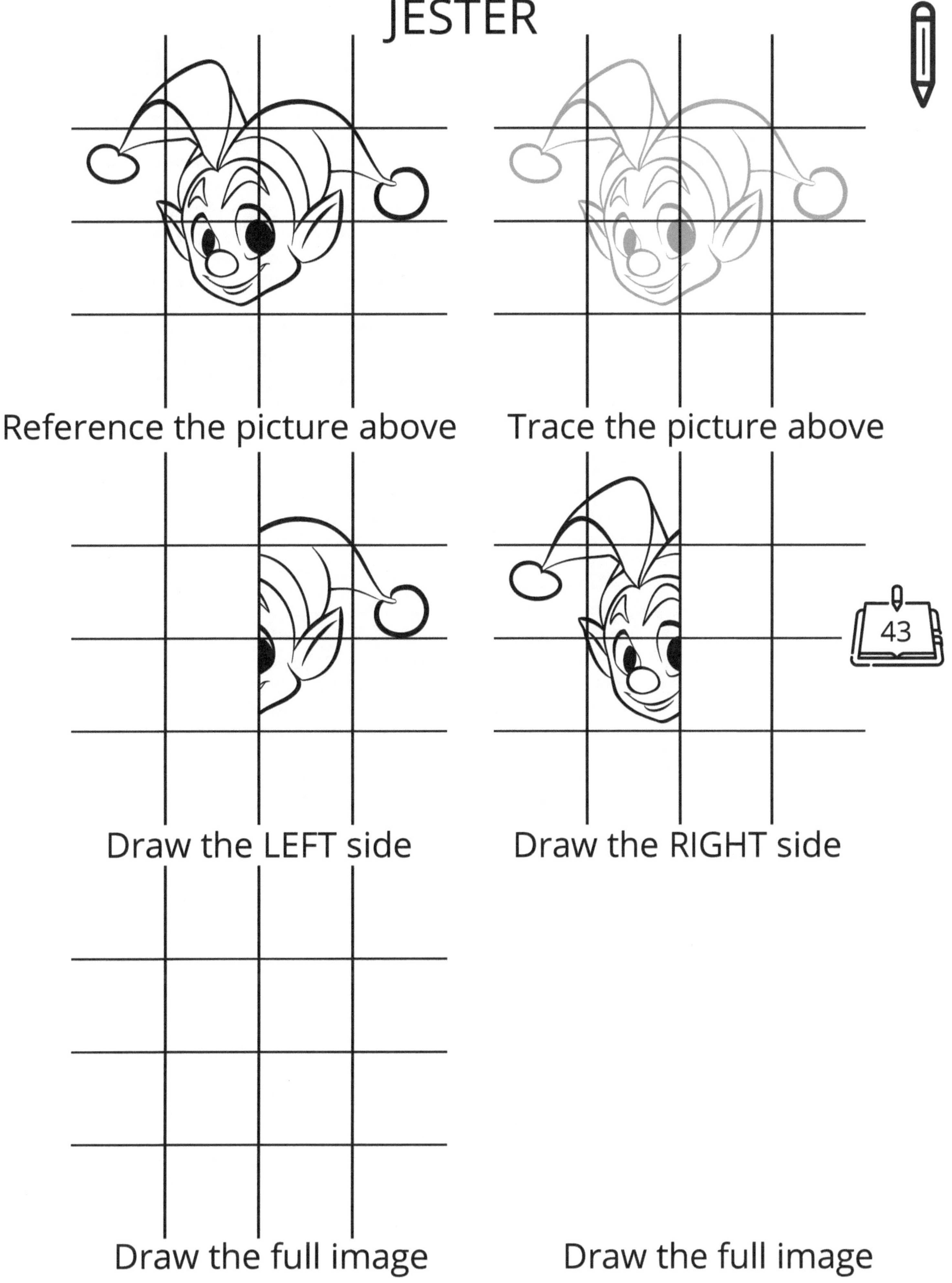
Reference the picture above
Trace the picture above
Draw the LEFT side
Draw the RIGHT side
Draw the full image
Draw the full image

MIMIC MOUTH

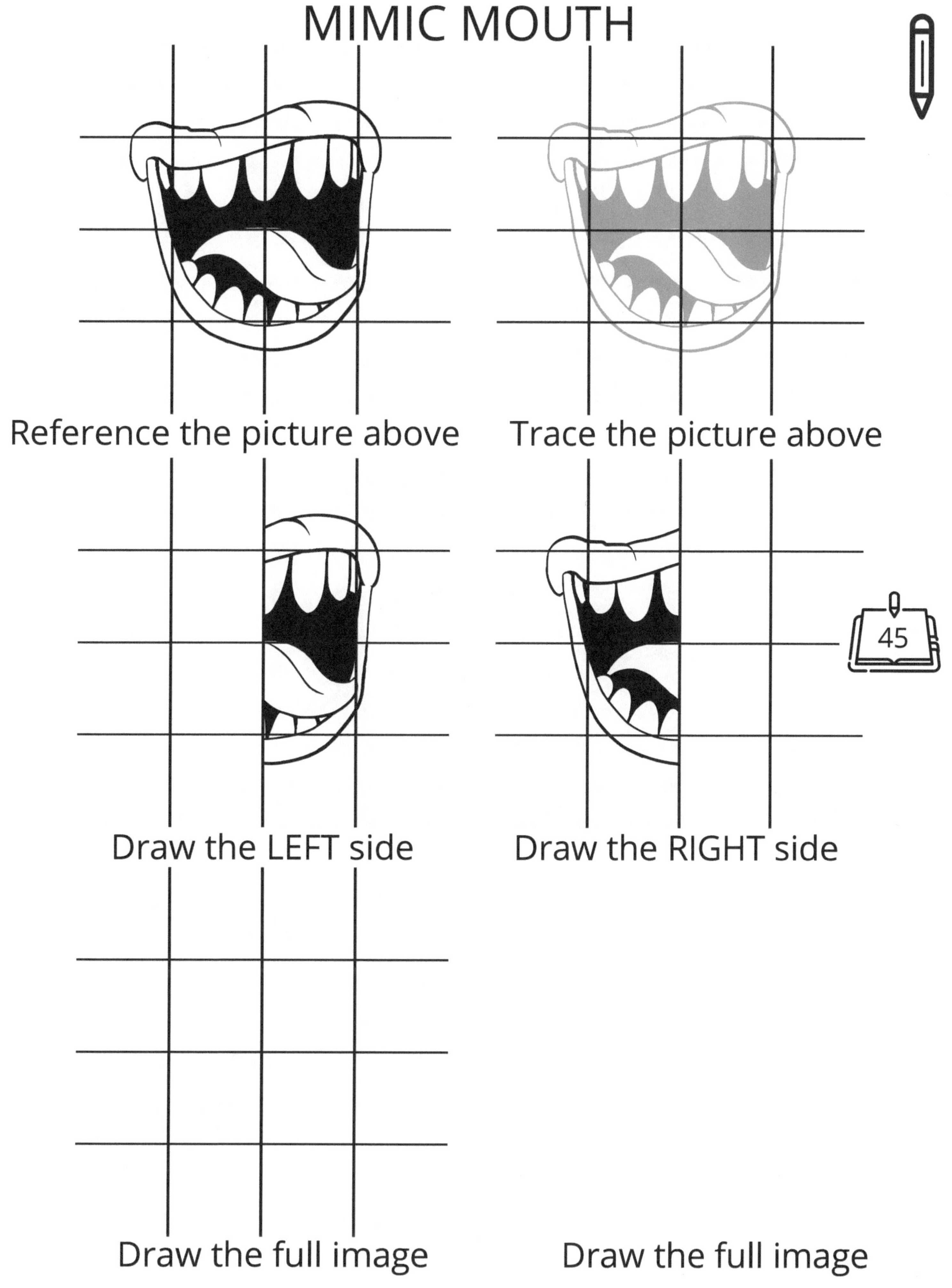
Reference the picture above
Trace the picture above
Draw the LEFT side
Draw the RIGHT side
Draw the full image
Draw the full image

MAGIC WAND

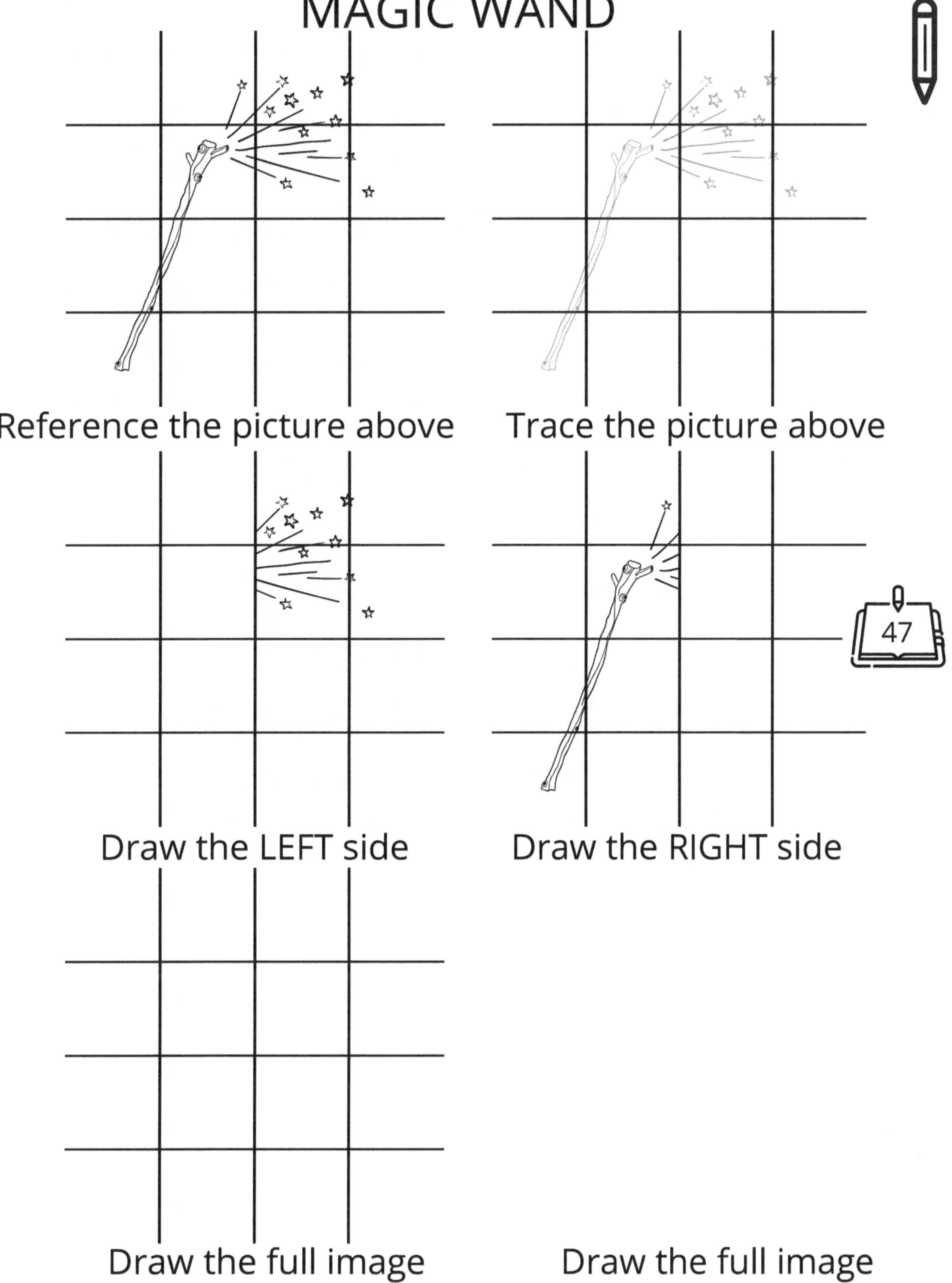
Reference the picture above
Trace the picture above
Draw the LEFT side
Draw the RIGHT side
Draw the full image
Draw the full image

MAGIC POTION

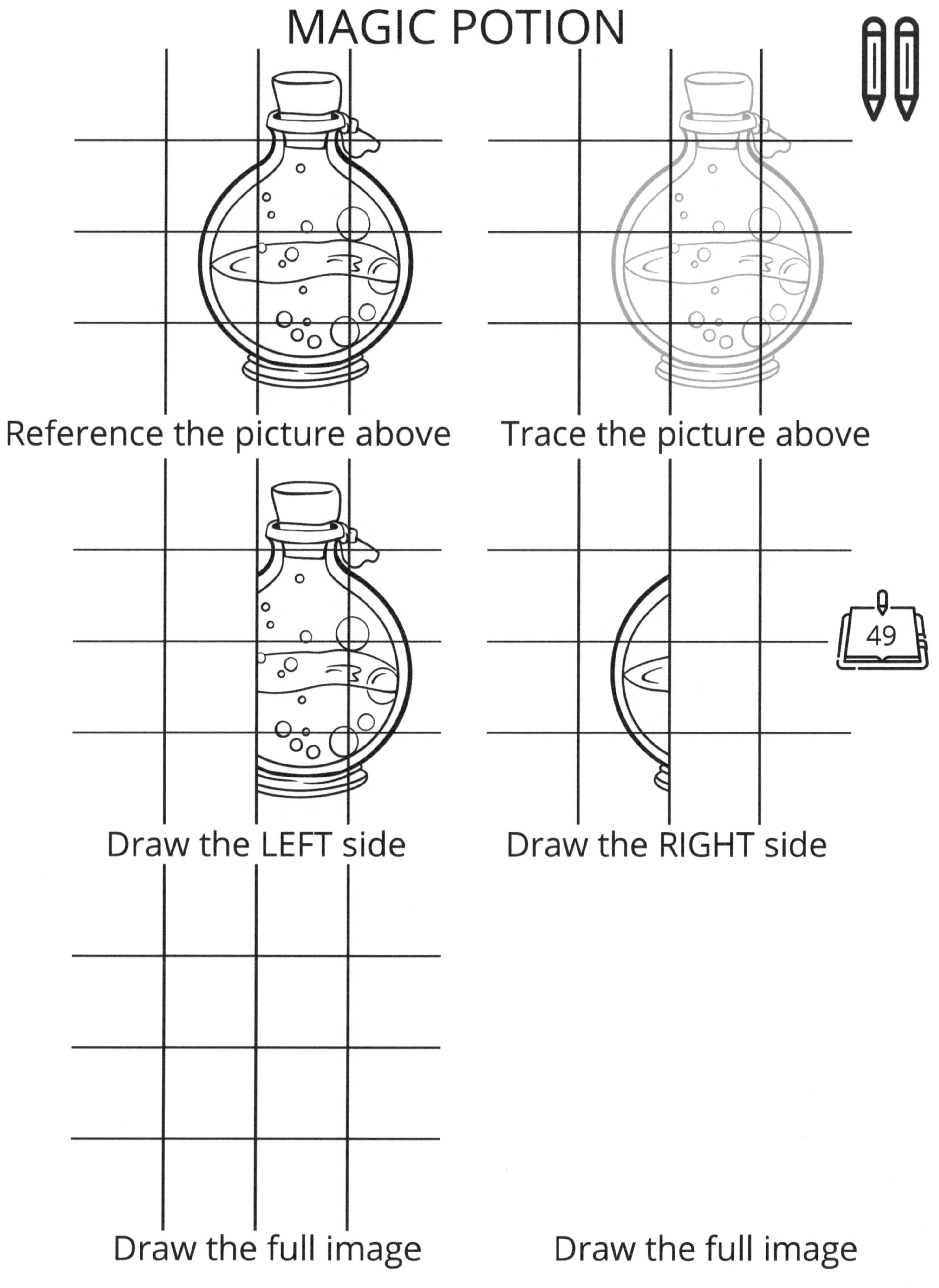

CRYSTAL BALL

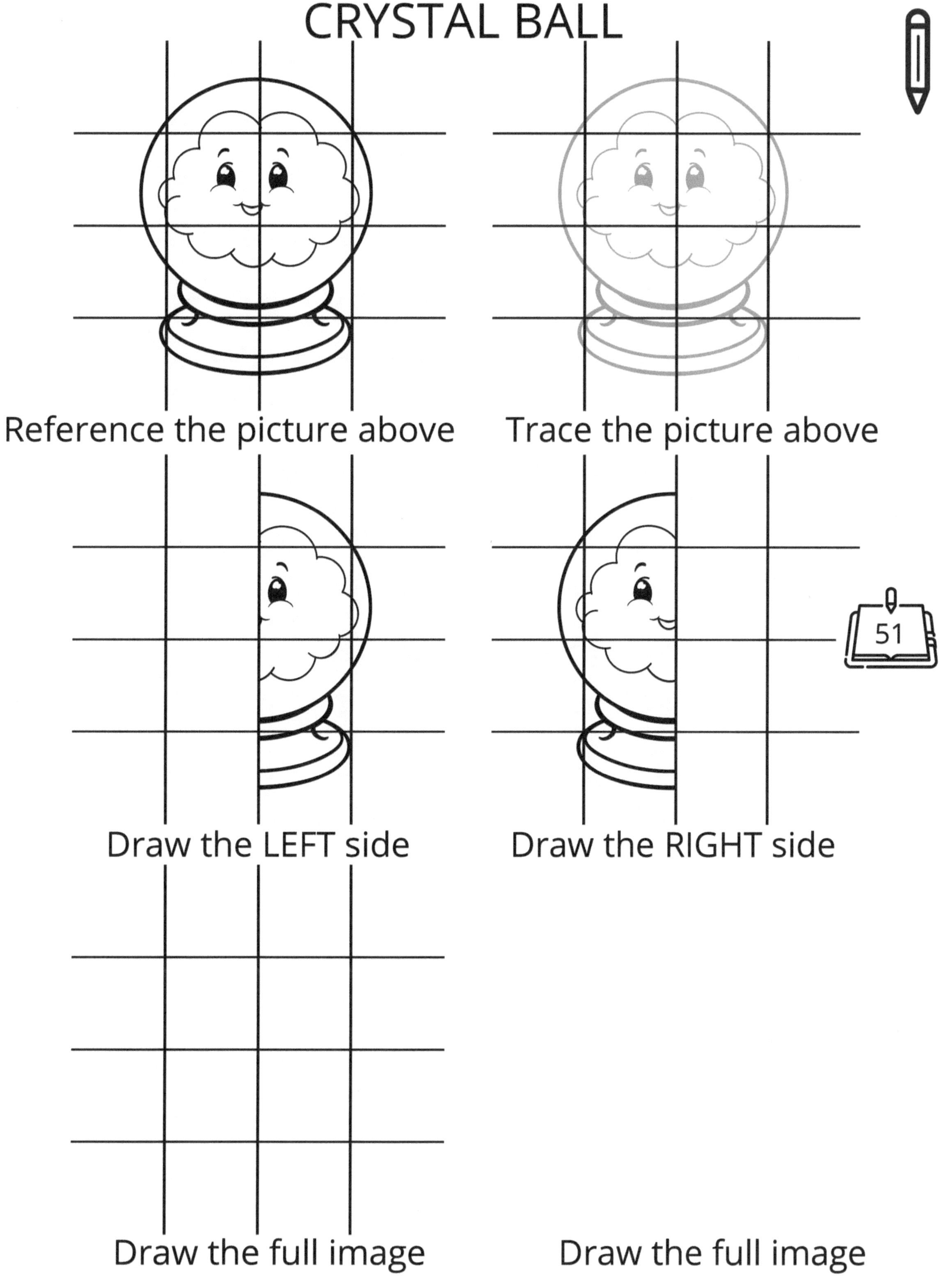

SPELL BOOK

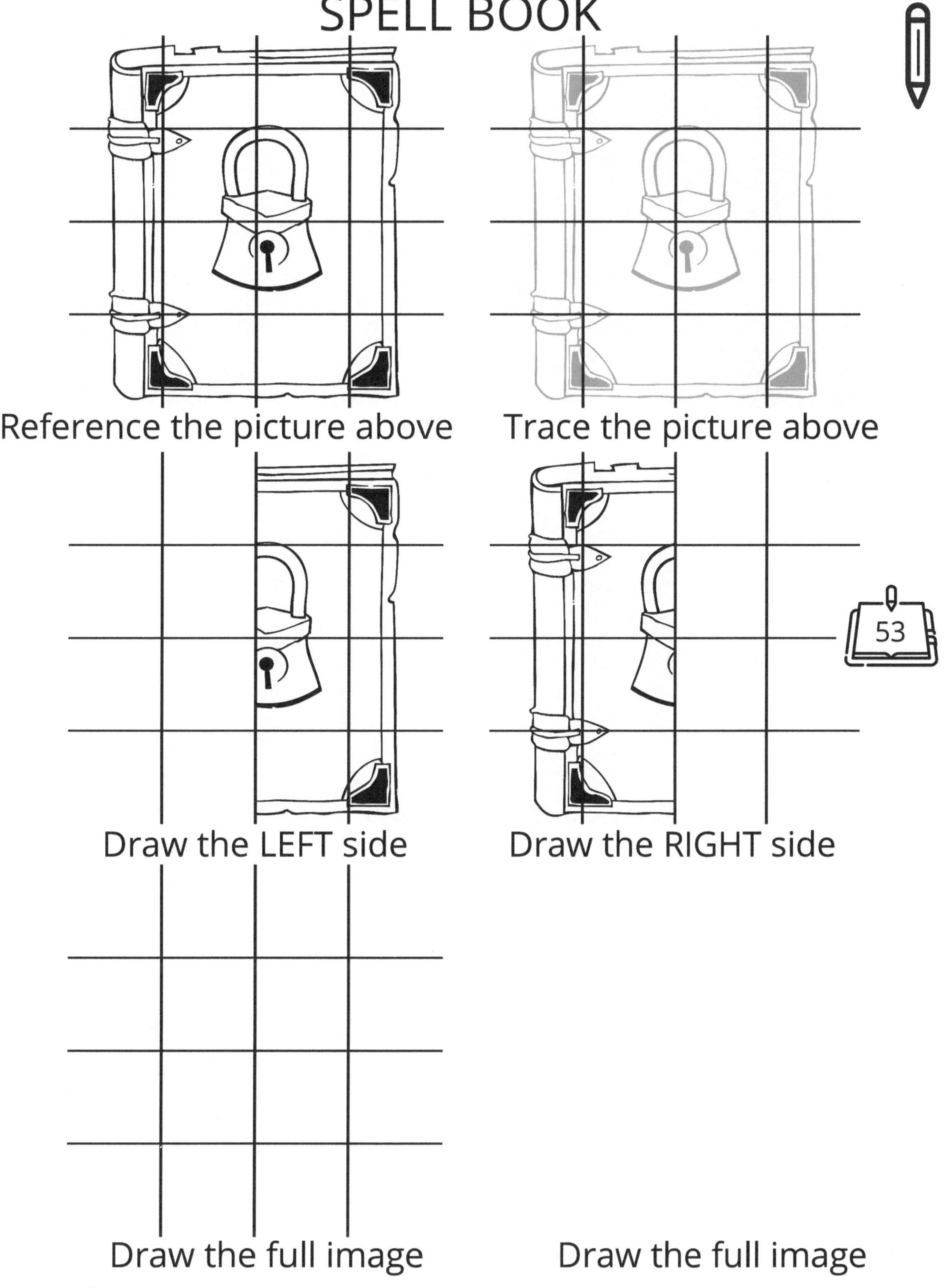

Reference the picture above
Trace the picture above
Draw the LEFT side
Draw the RIGHT side
Draw the full image
Draw the full image

GRIFFIN

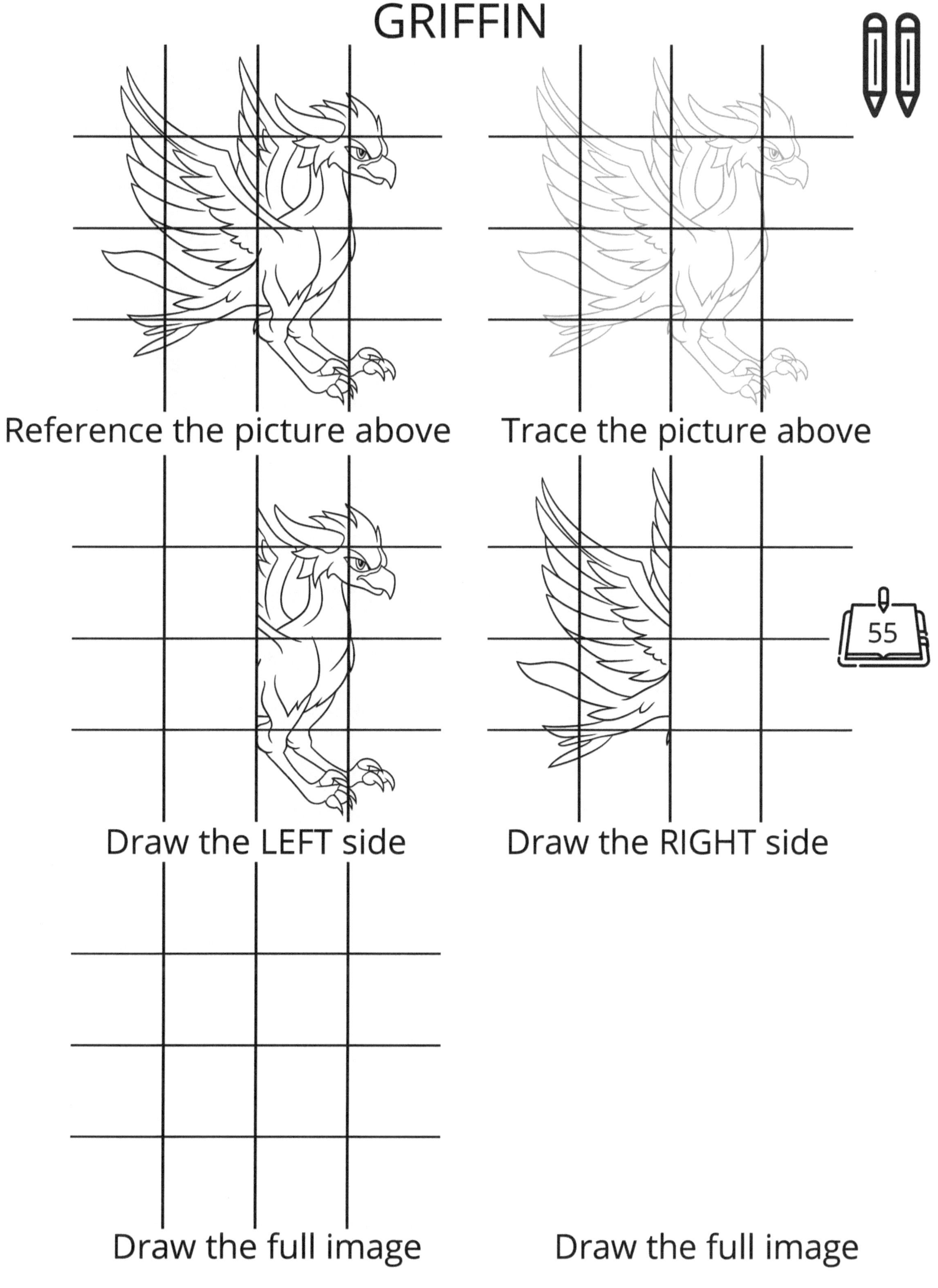
Reference the picture above
Trace the picture above
Draw the LEFT side
Draw the RIGHT side
55
Draw the full image
Draw the full image

UNICORN

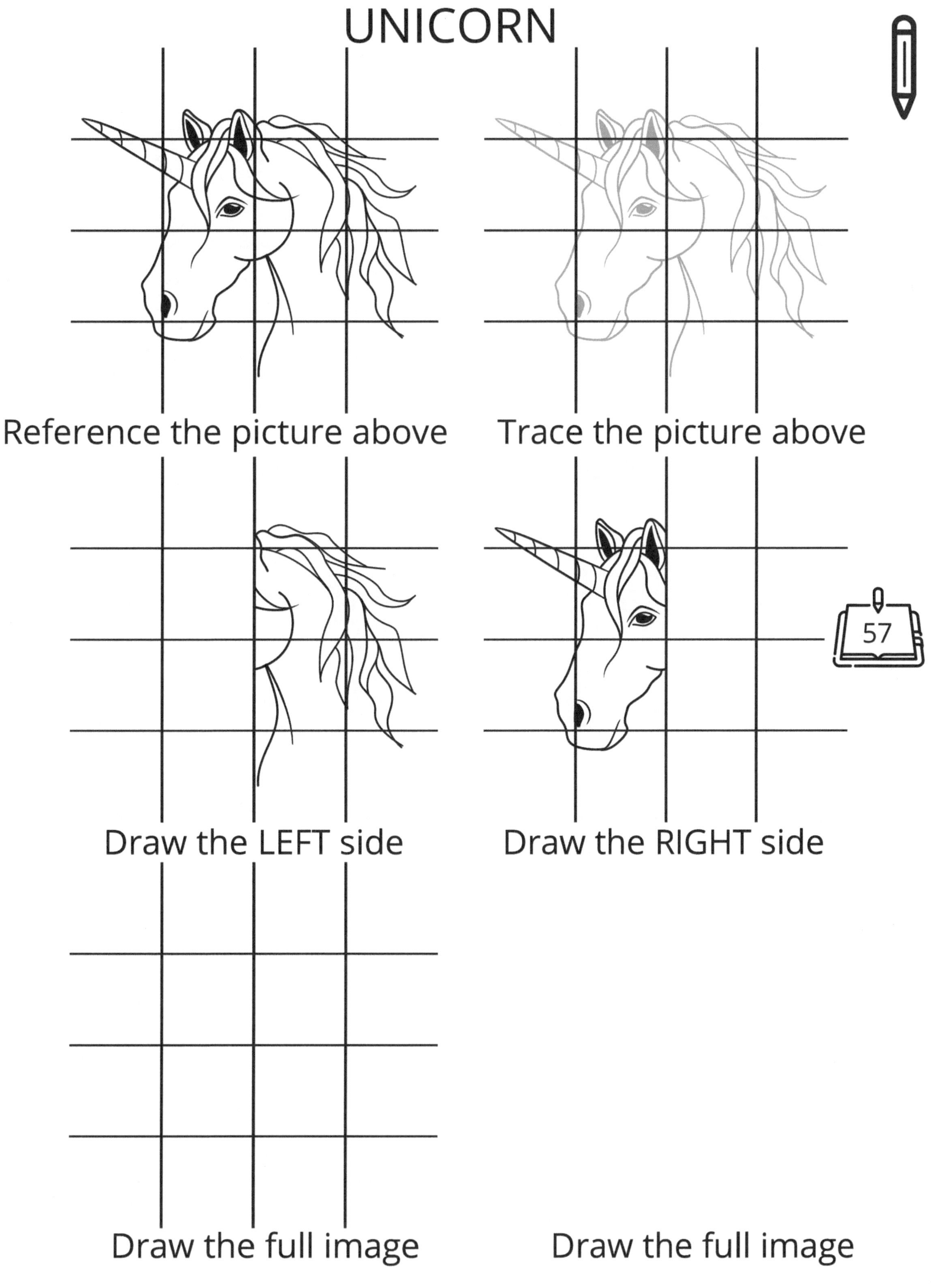
Reference the picture above
Trace the picture above
Draw the LEFT side
Draw the RIGHT side
57
Draw the full image
Draw the full image

FAIRY

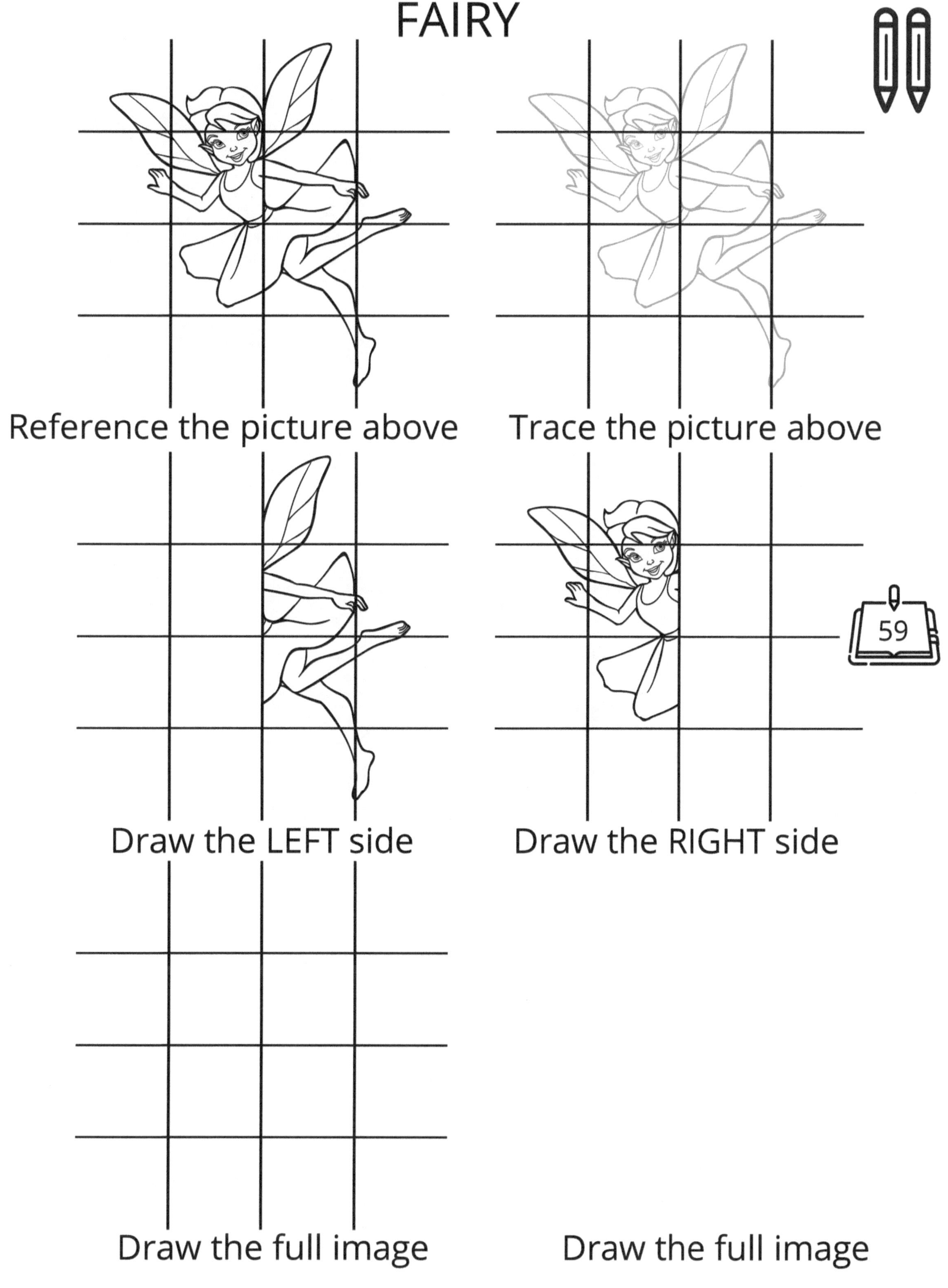

Reference the picture above
Trace the picture above
Draw the LEFT side
Draw the RIGHT side
59
Draw the full image
Draw the full image

GNOME

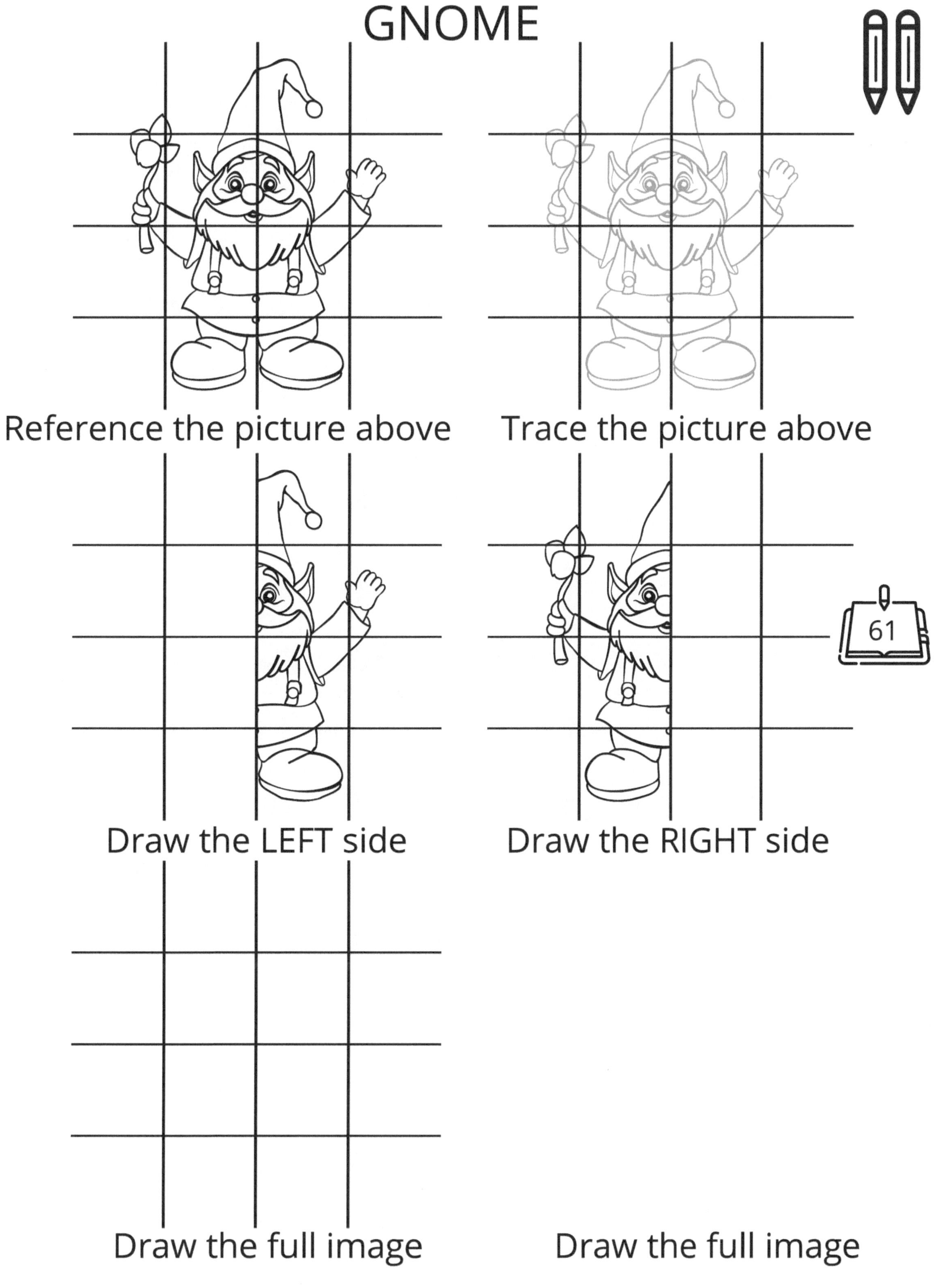
Reference the picture above
Trace the picture above
Draw the LEFT side
Draw the RIGHT side
Draw the full image
Draw the full image

DRAGON

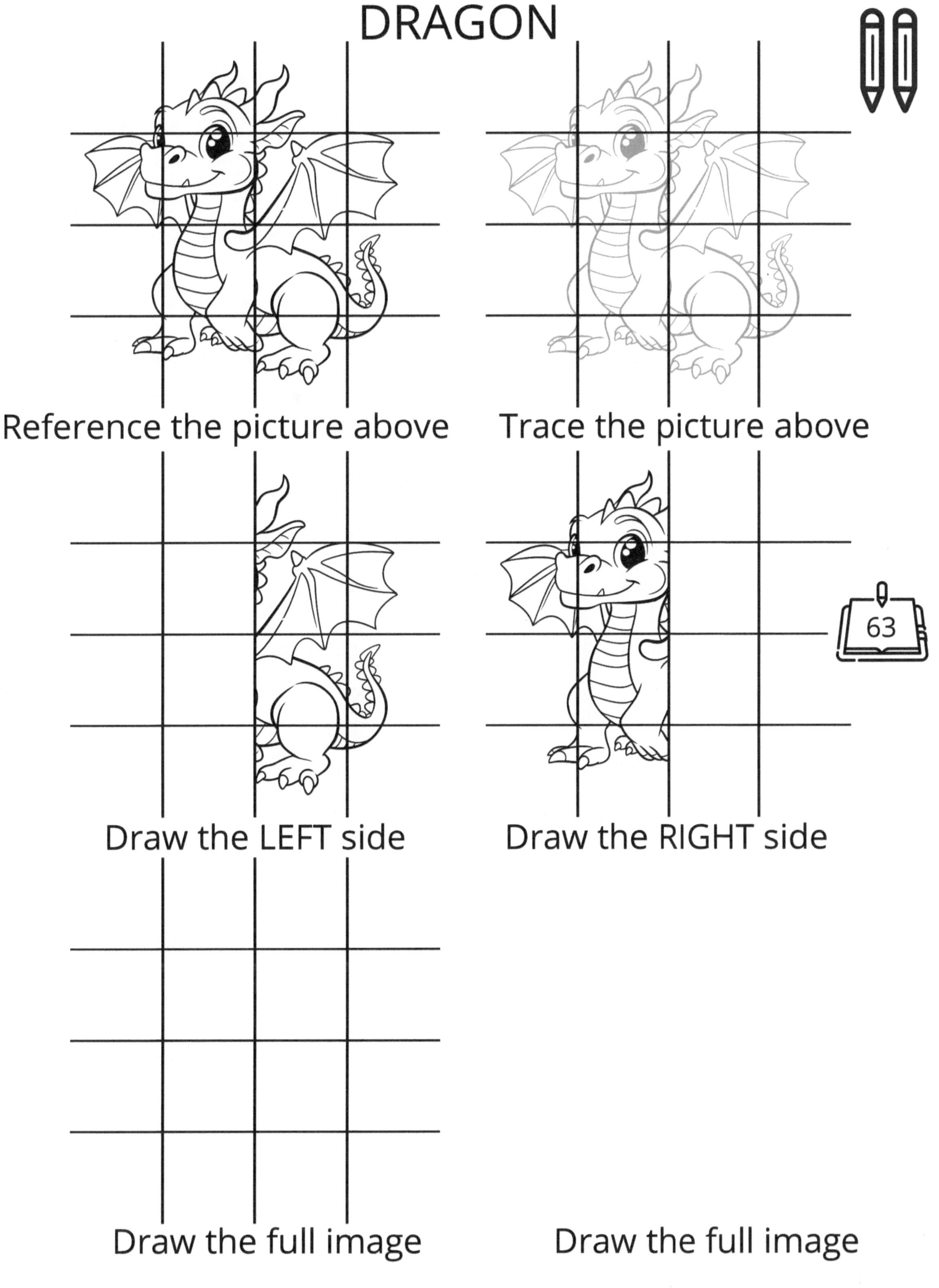
Reference the picture above
Trace the picture above
Draw the LEFT side
Draw the RIGHT side
63
Draw the full image
Draw the full image

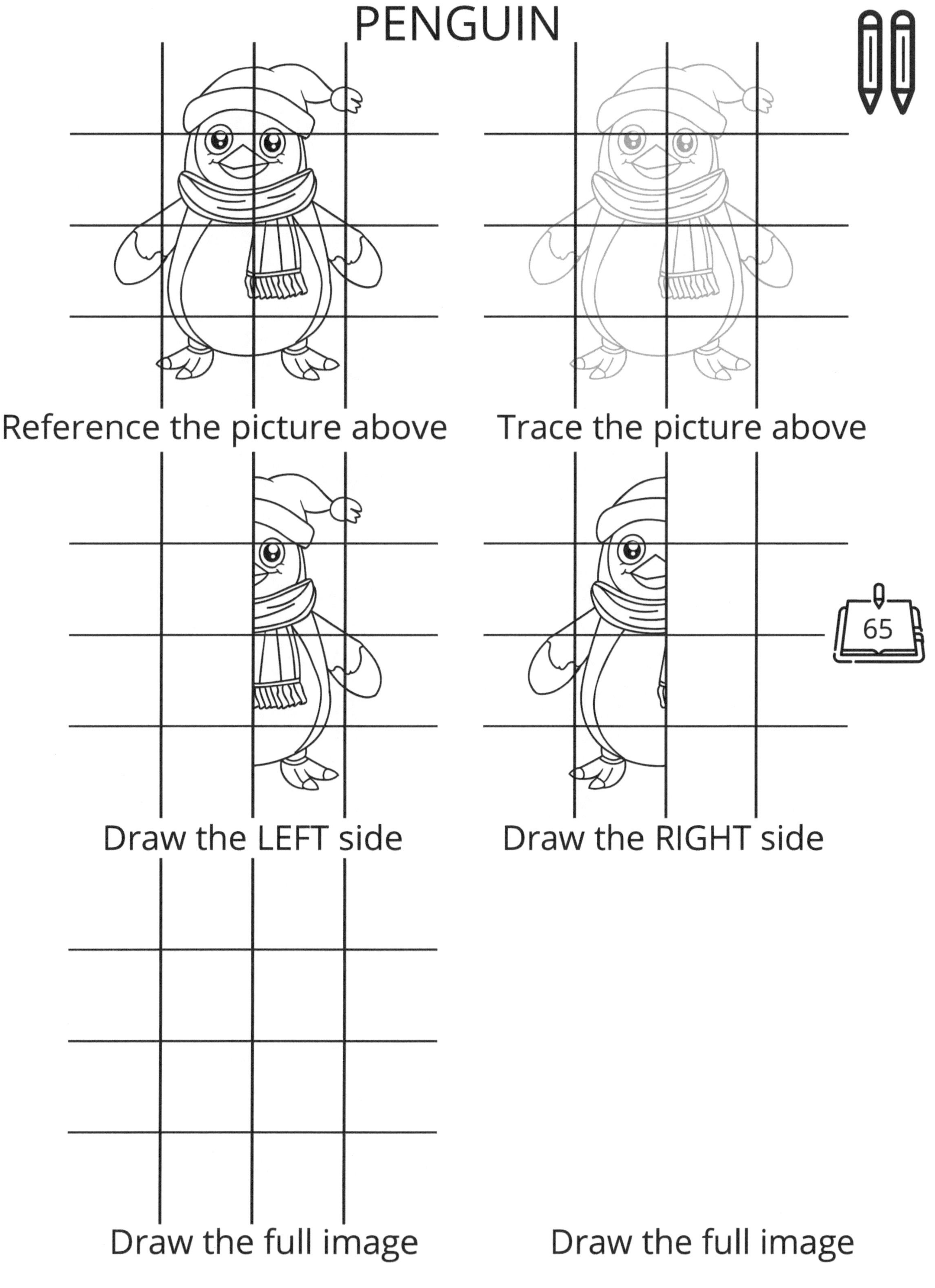
PENGUIN
Reference the picture above
Trace the picture above
Draw the LEFT side
Draw the RIGHT side
Draw the full image
Draw the full image
65

KITTEN

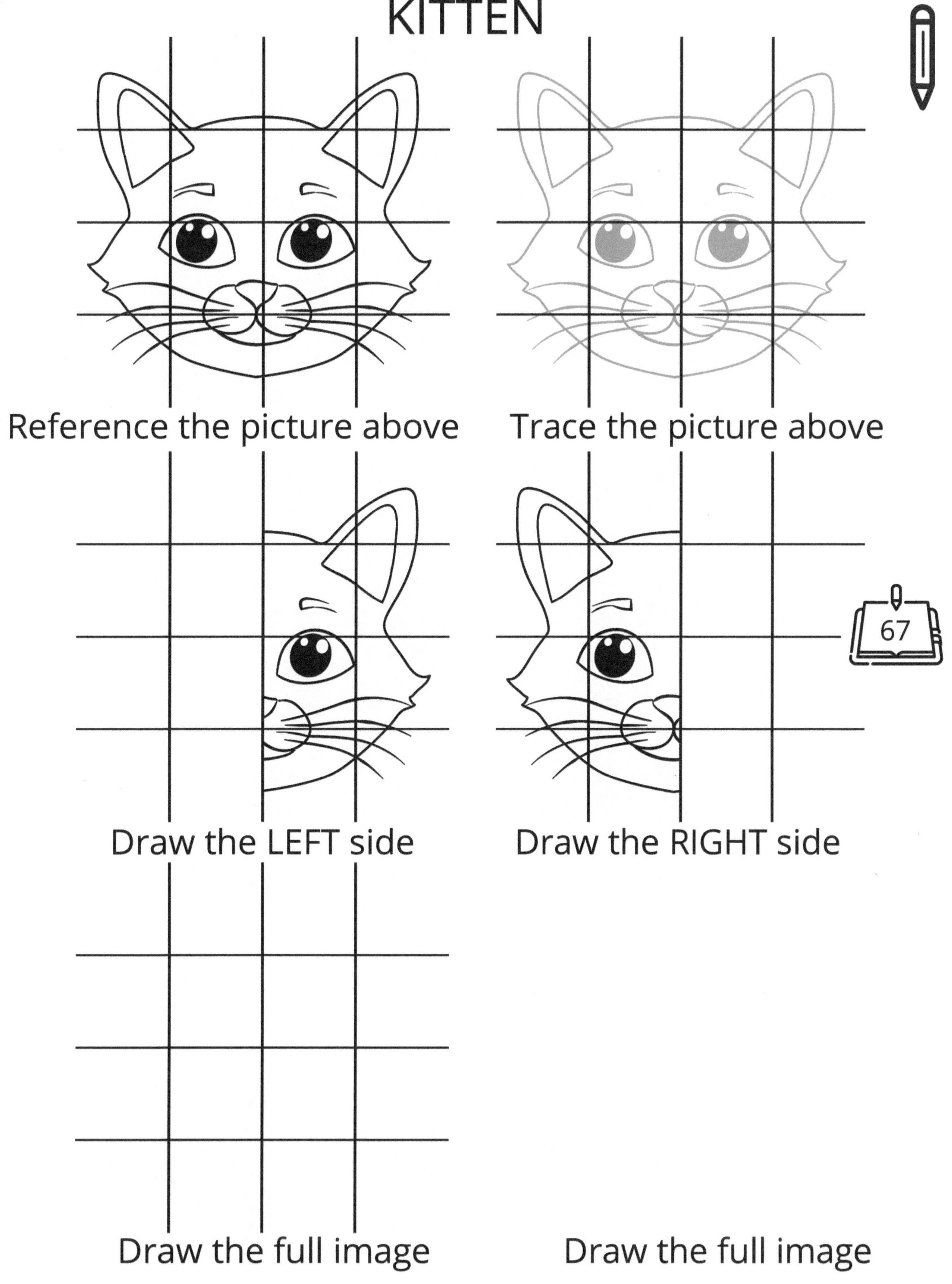
Reference the picture above
Trace the picture above
Draw the LEFT side
Draw the RIGHT side
67
Draw the full image
Draw the full image

TEDDY BEAR

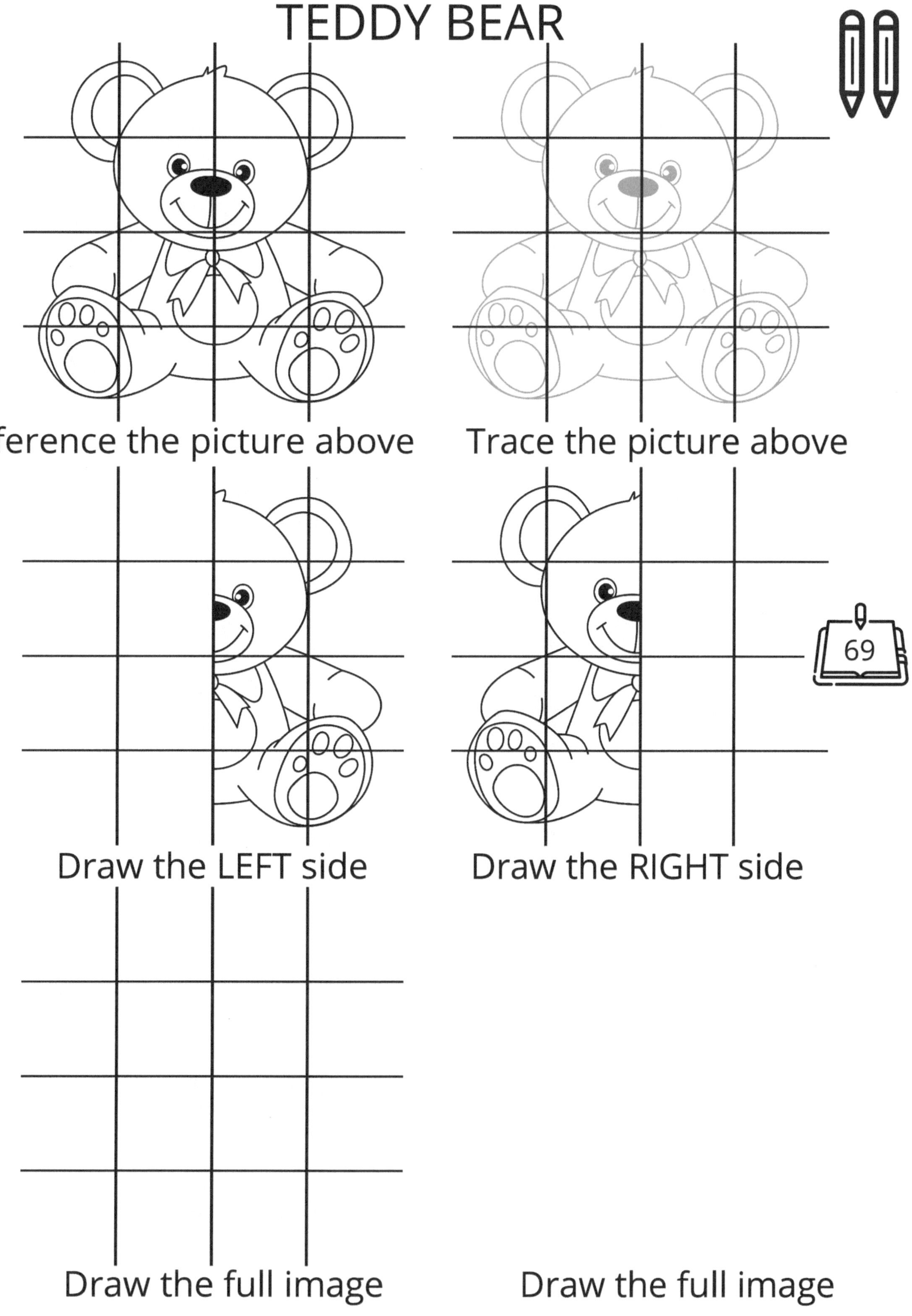
Reference the picture above
Trace the picture above
Draw the LEFT side
Draw the RIGHT side
Draw the full image
Draw the full image

BUNNY

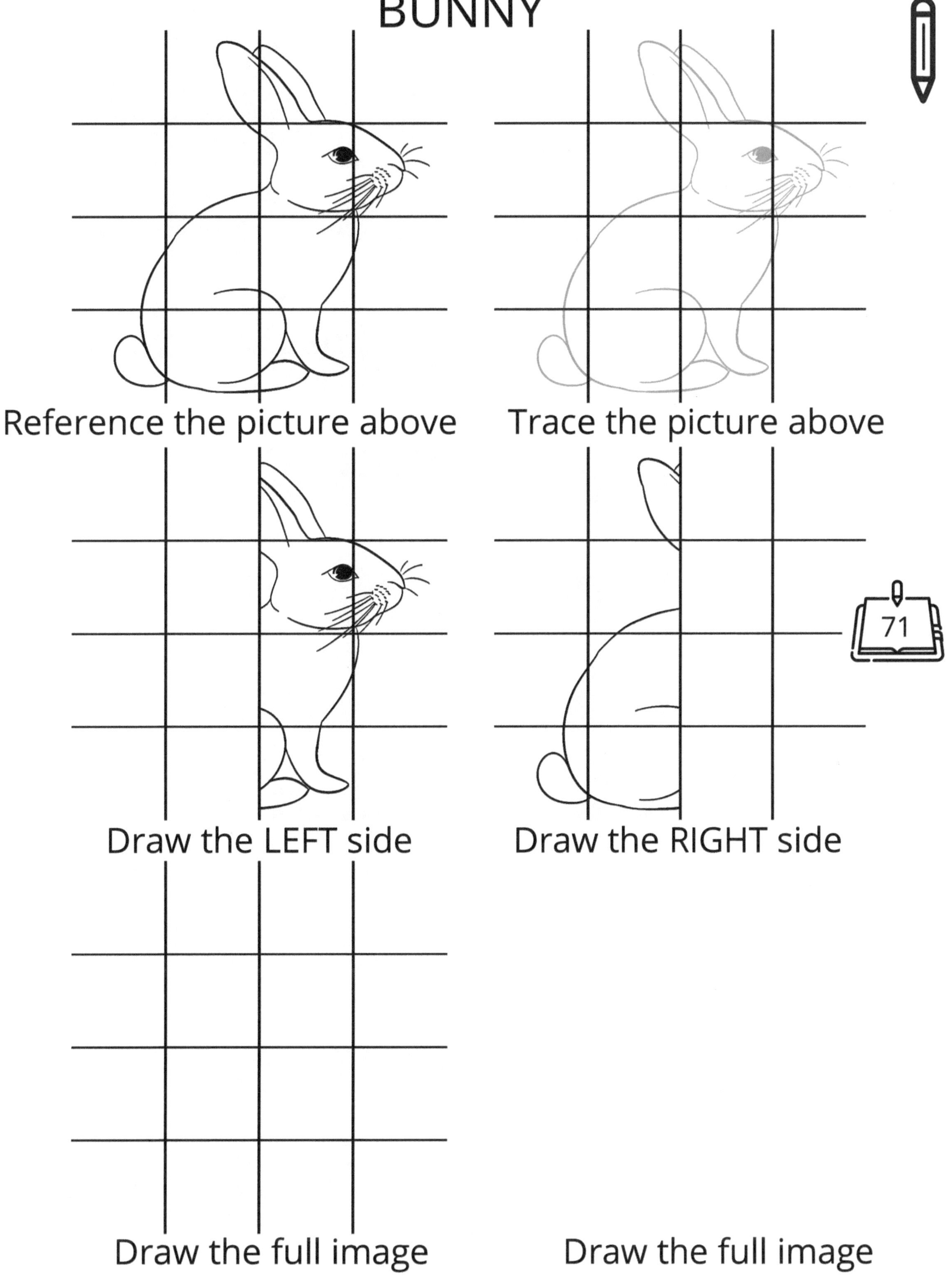

Reference the picture above
Trace the picture above
Draw the LEFT side
Draw the RIGHT side
71
Draw the full image
Draw the full image

RUBBER DUCKY

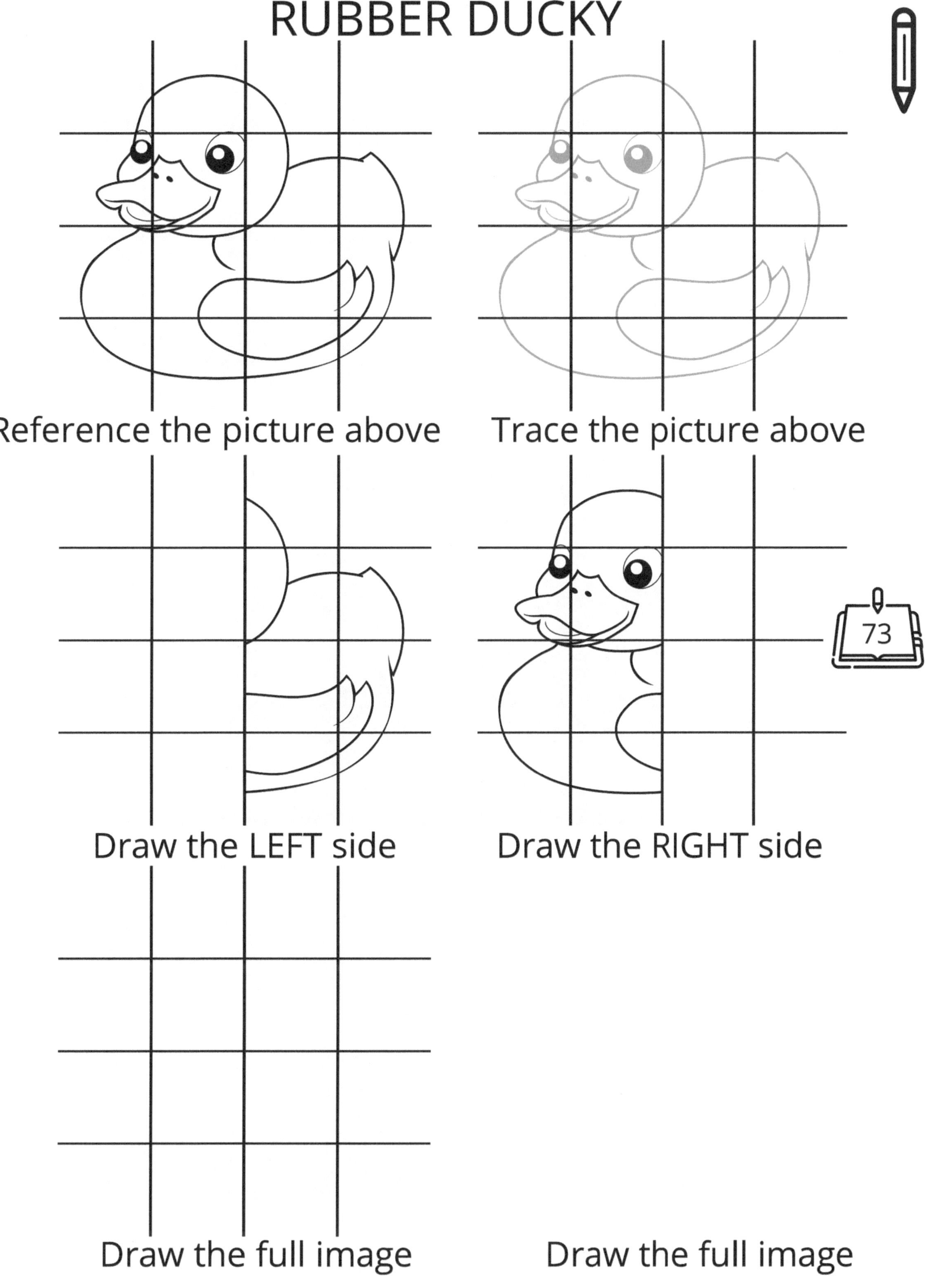

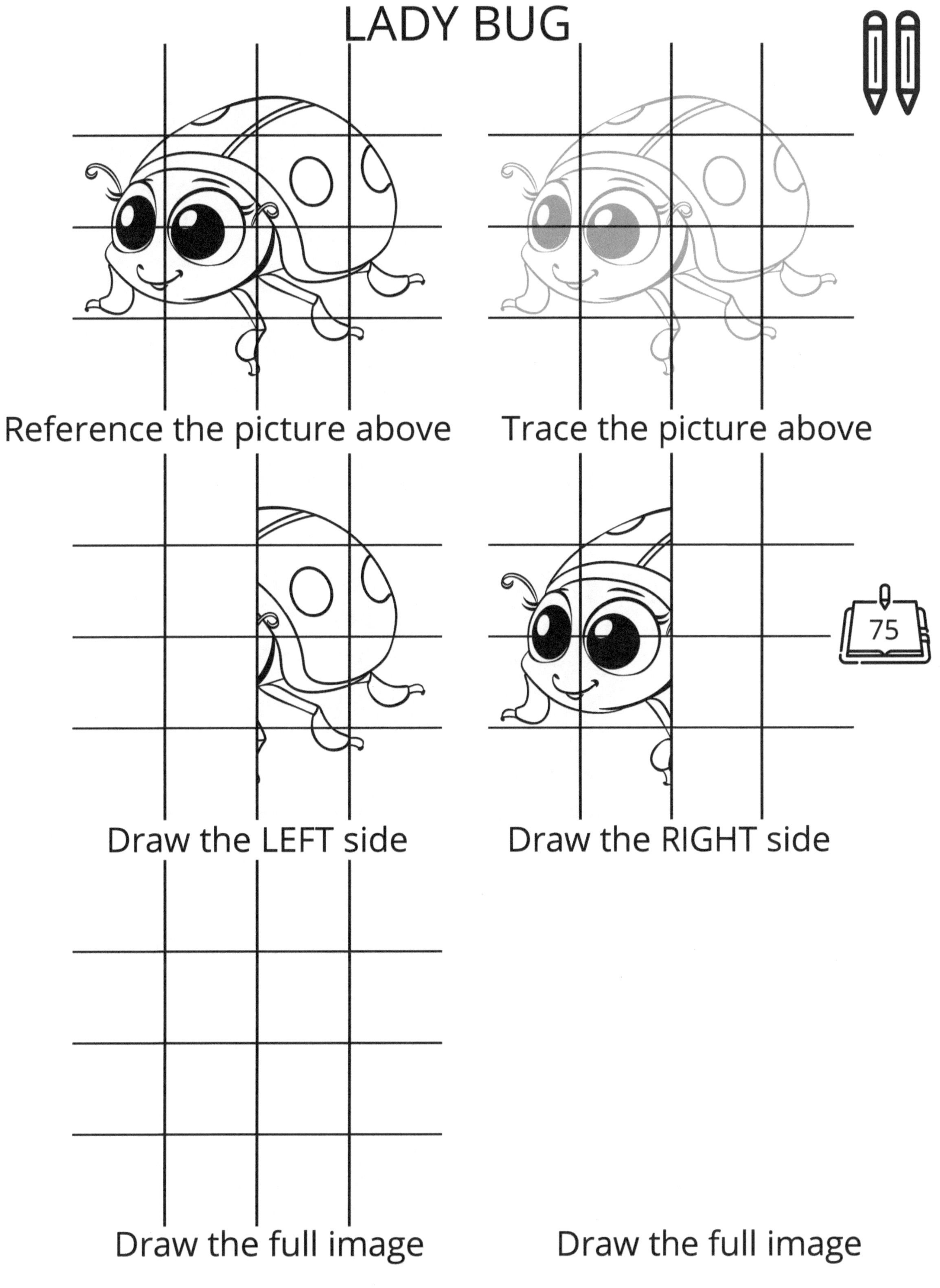
LADY BUG
Reference the picture above
Trace the picture above
Draw the LEFT side
Draw the RIGHT side
Draw the full image
Draw the full image
75

BUTTERFLY

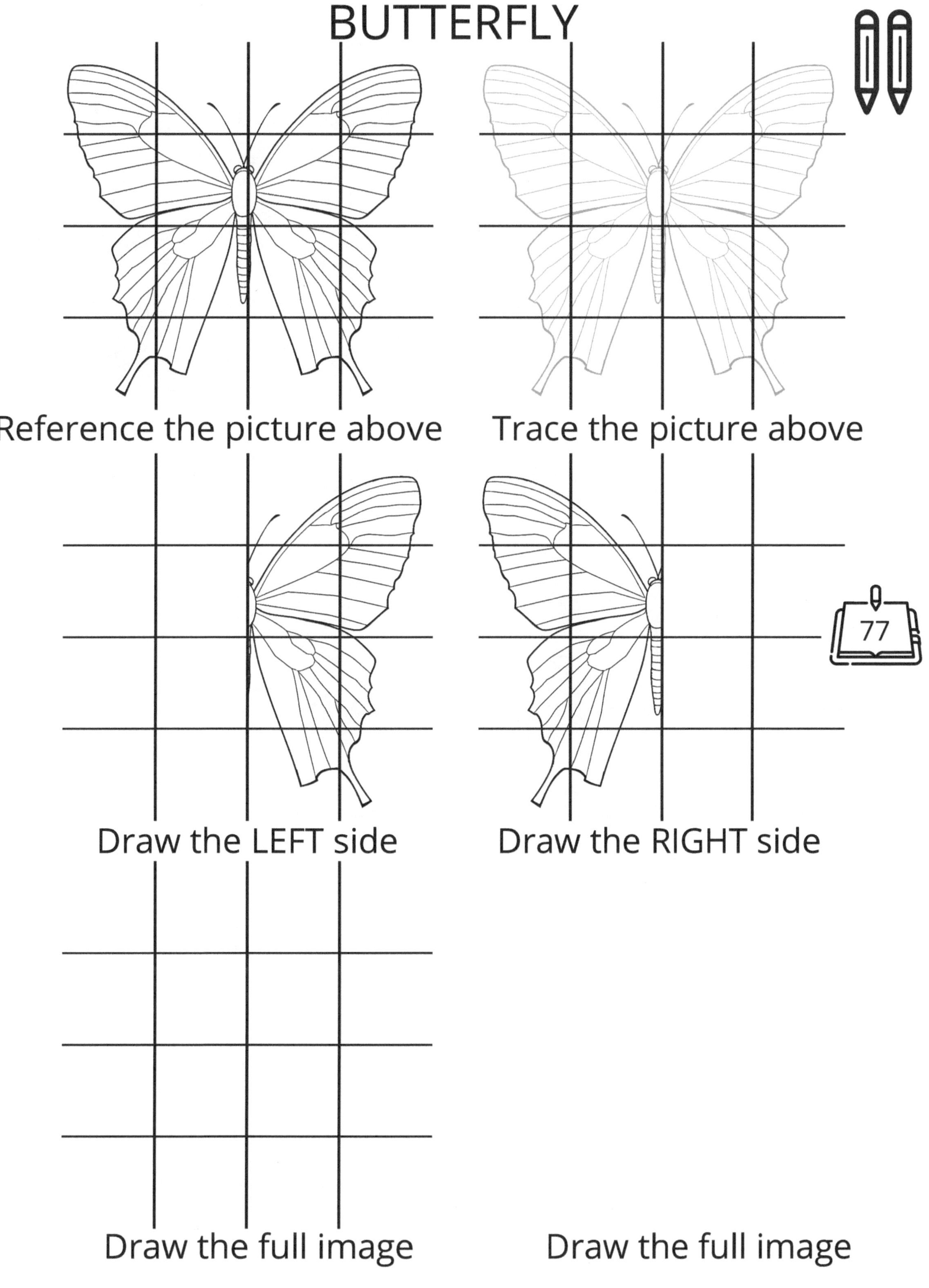
Reference the picture above
Trace the picture above
77
Draw the LEFT side
Draw the RIGHT side
Draw the full image
Draw the full image

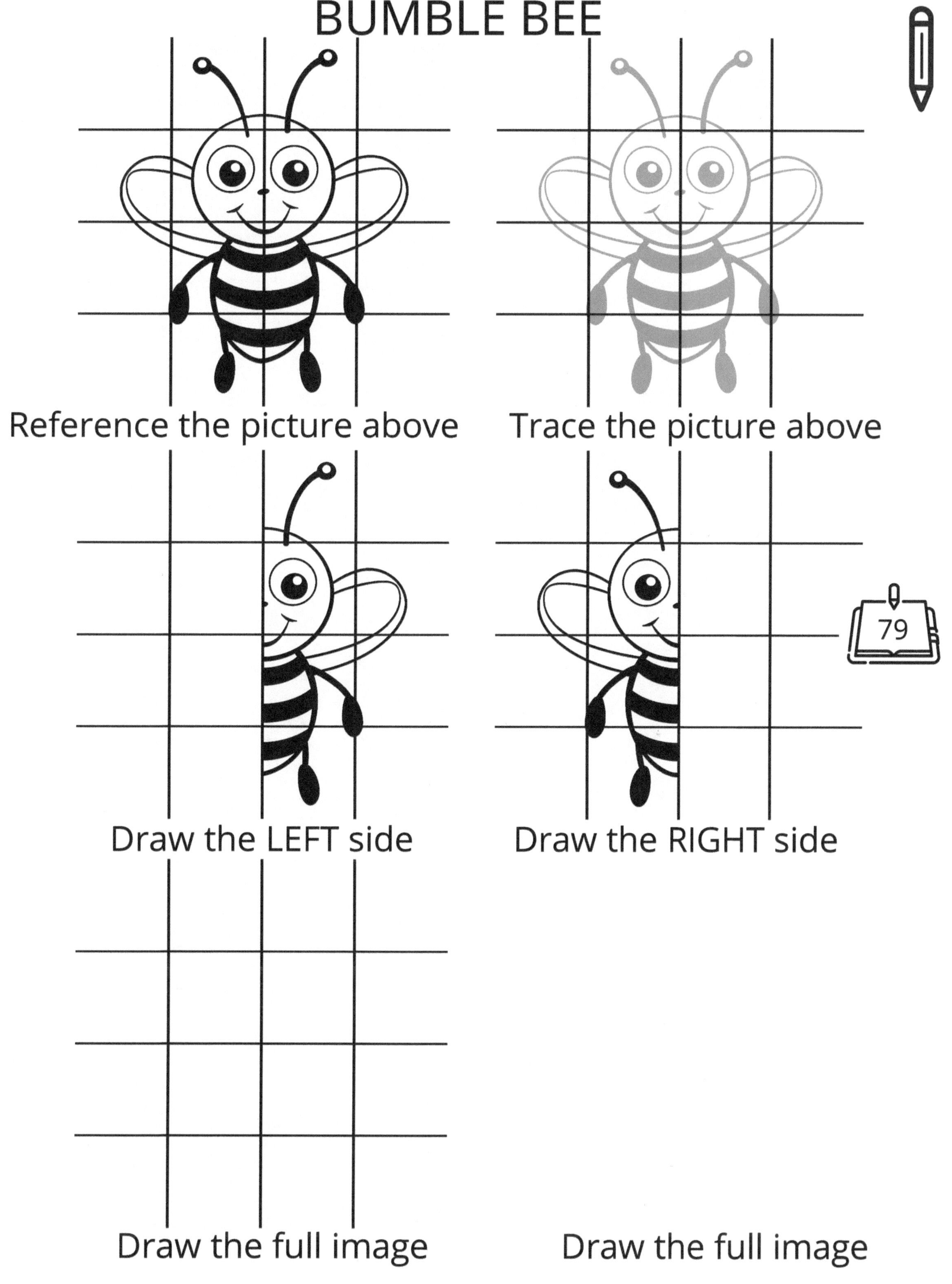
BUMBLE BEE
Reference the picture above
Trace the picture above
Draw the LEFT side
Draw the RIGHT side
Draw the full image
Draw the full image

FROG

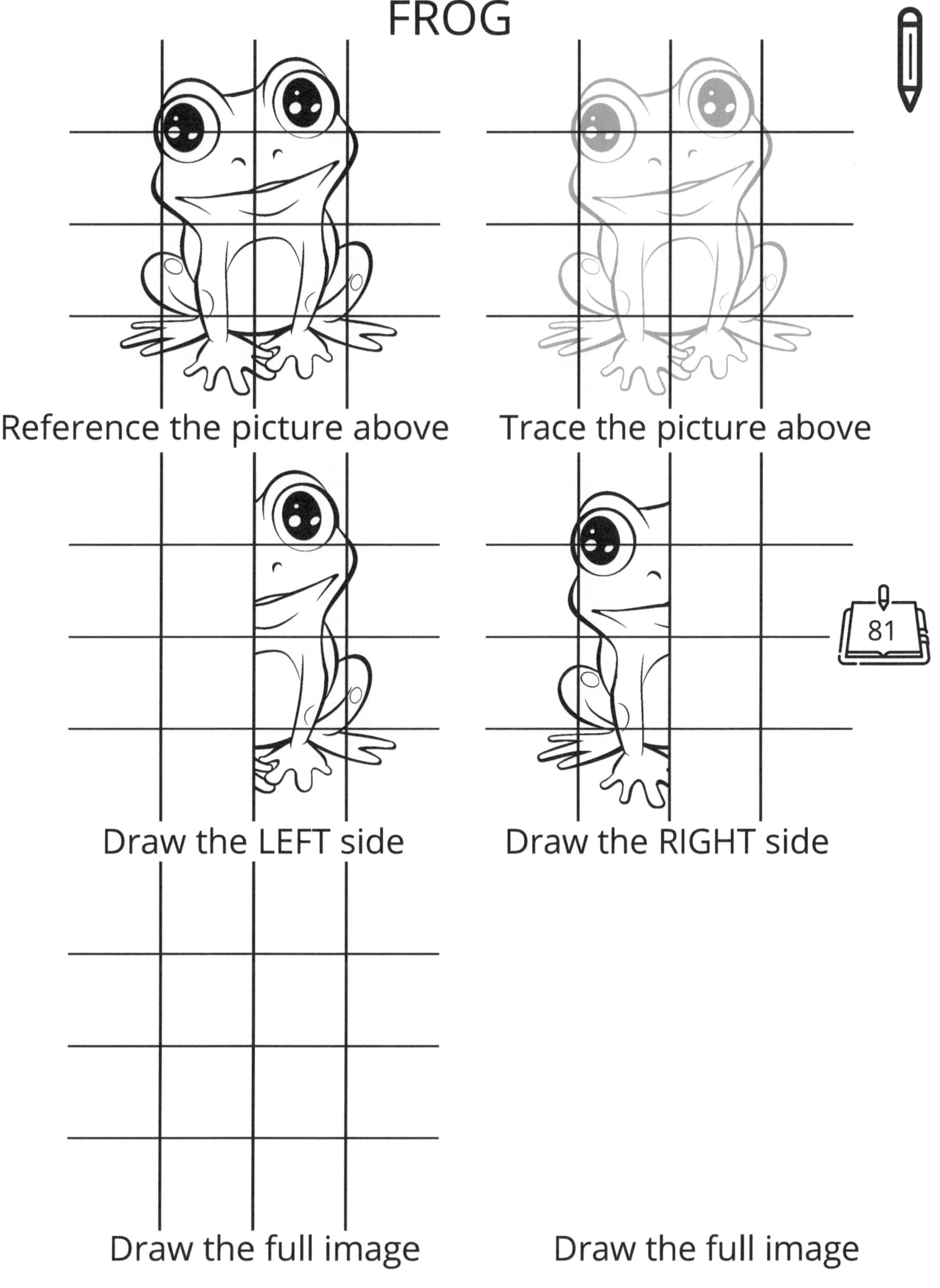
Reference the picture above
Trace the picture above
Draw the LEFT side
Draw the RIGHT side
Draw the full image
Draw the full image

MOTH

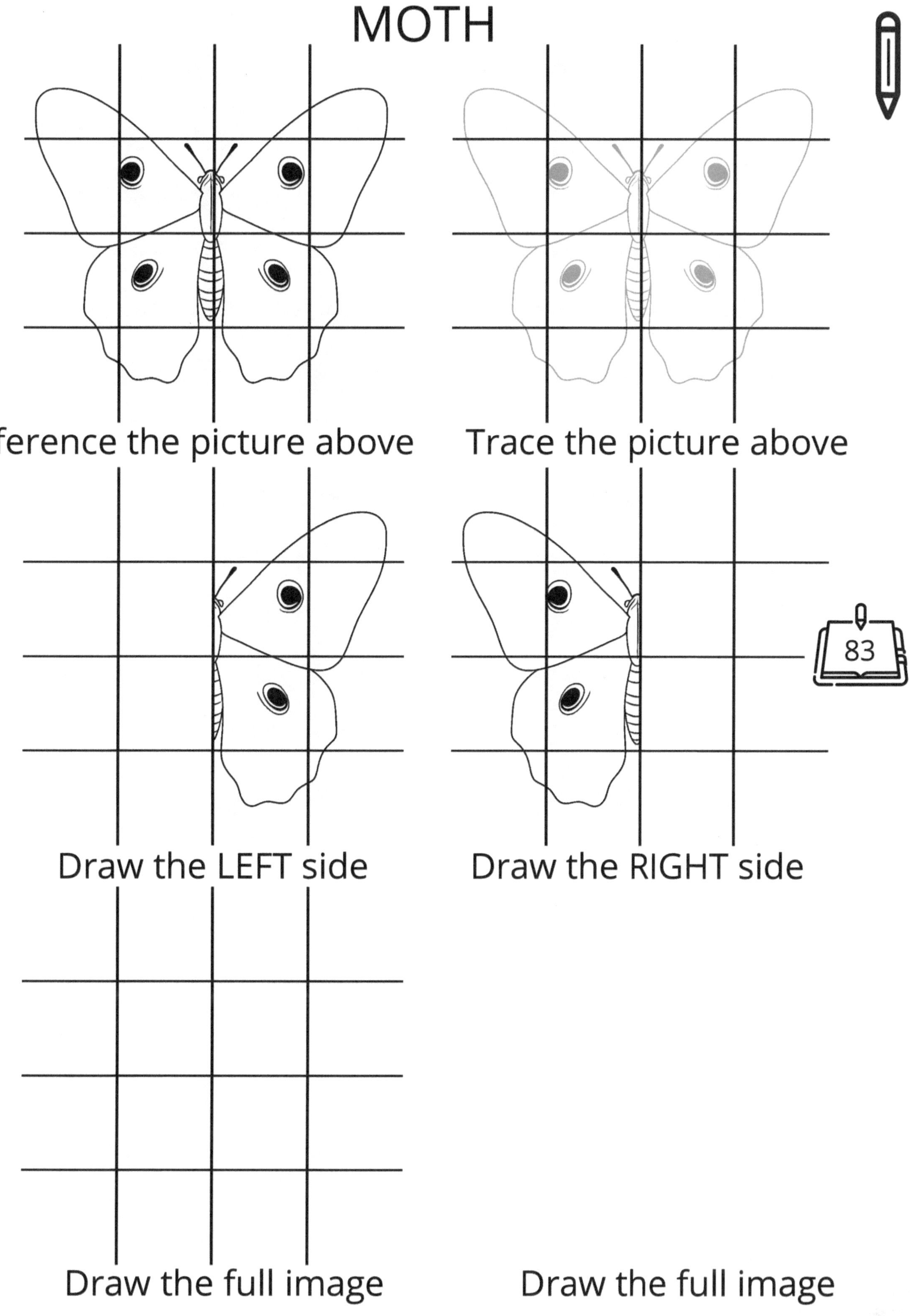

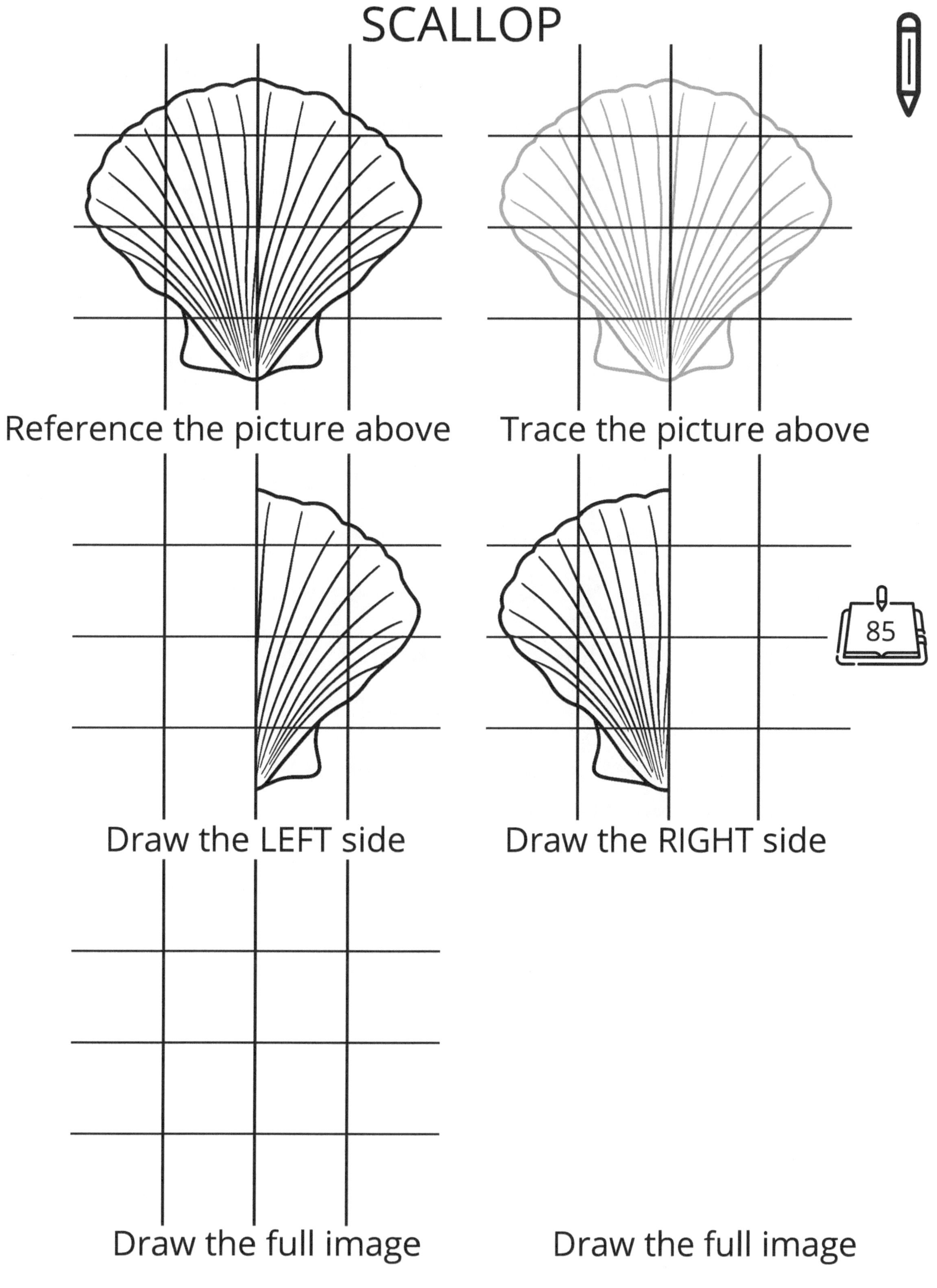
SCALLOP
Reference the picture above
Trace the picture above
Draw the LEFT side
Draw the RIGHT side
85
Draw the full image
Draw the full image

STARFISH

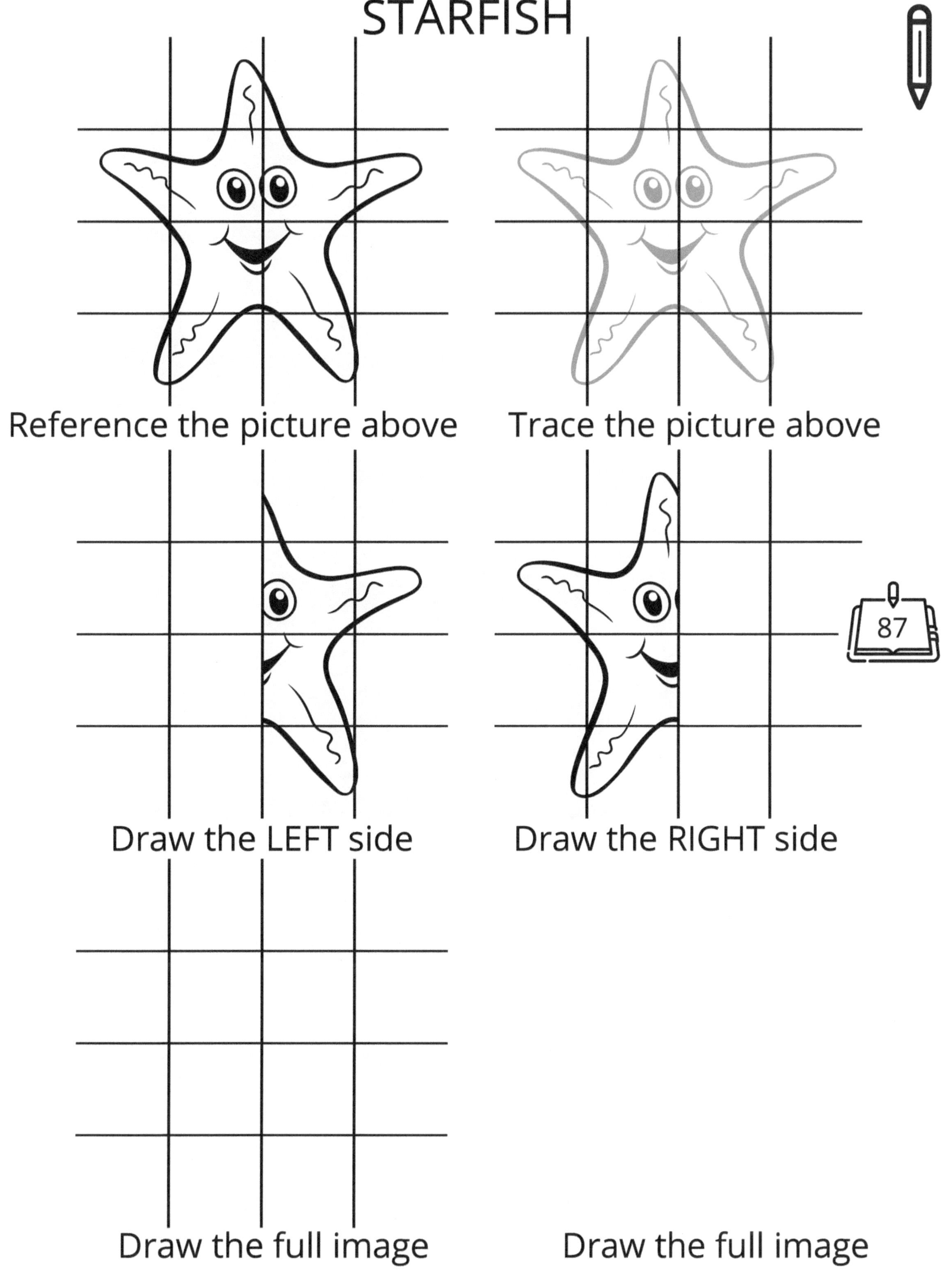

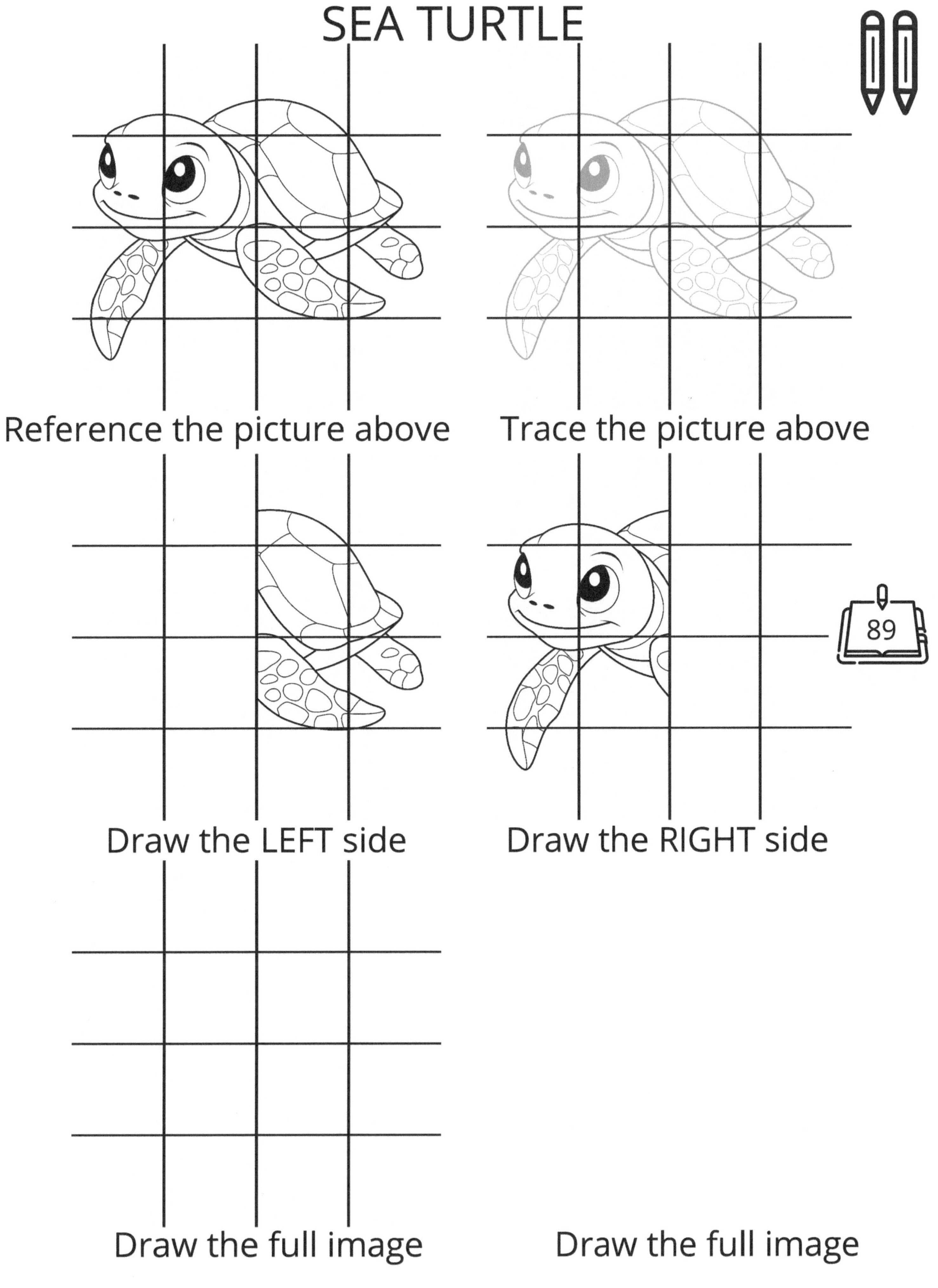
SEA TURTLE
Reference the picture above
Trace the picture above
Draw the LEFT side
Draw the RIGHT side
89
Draw the full image
Draw the full image

SURF BOARD

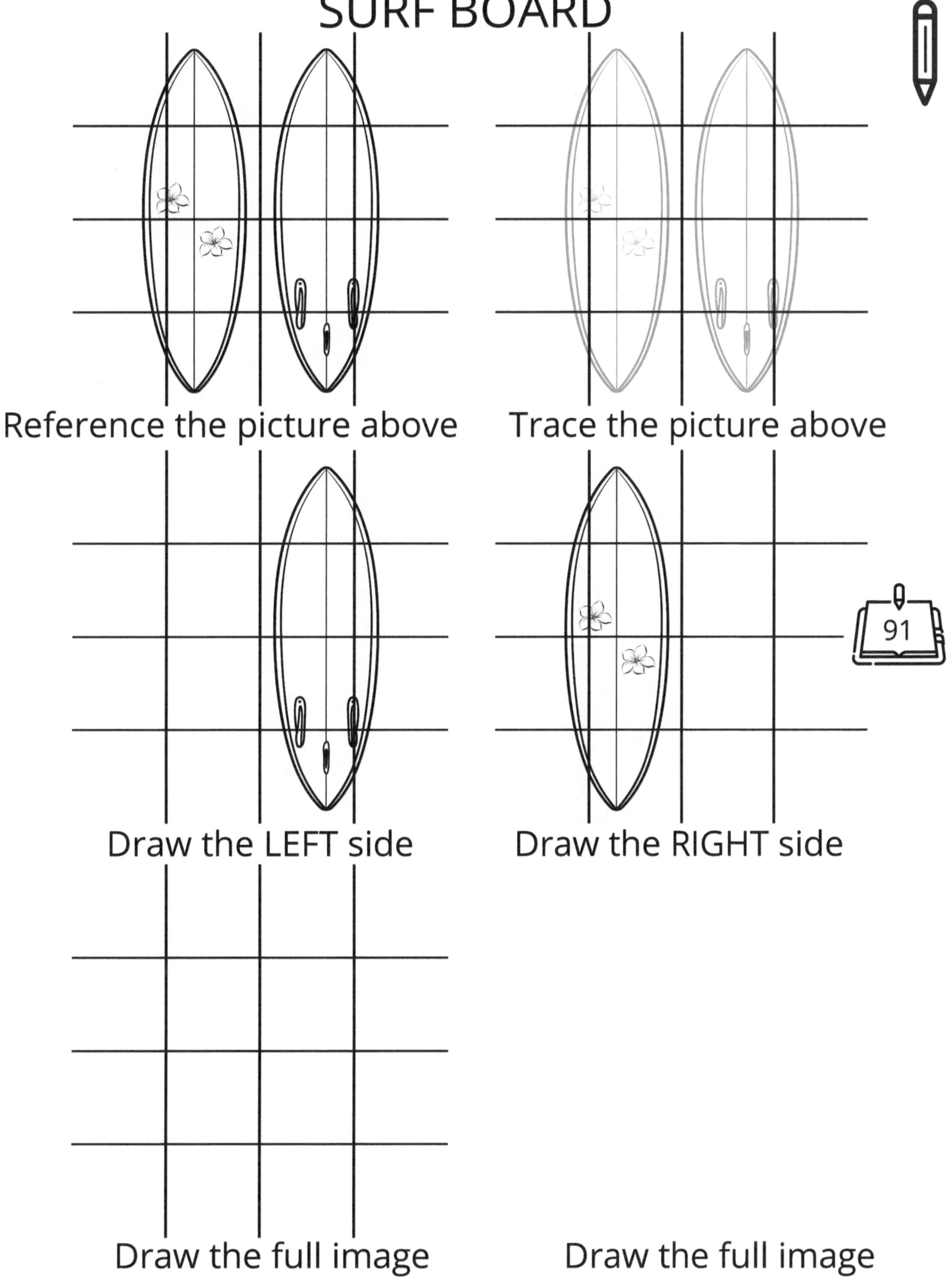

LIGHTHOUSE

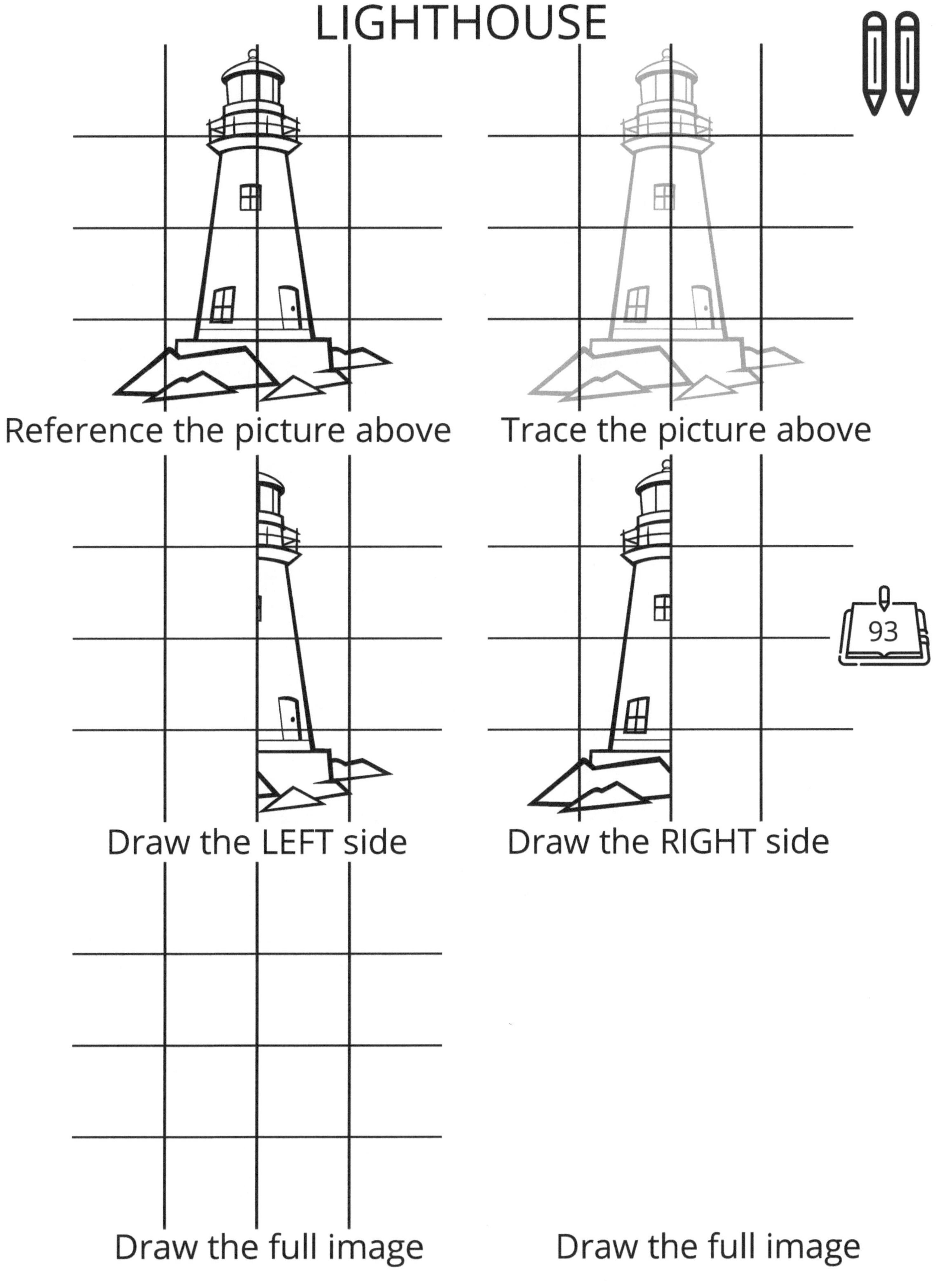

SWING

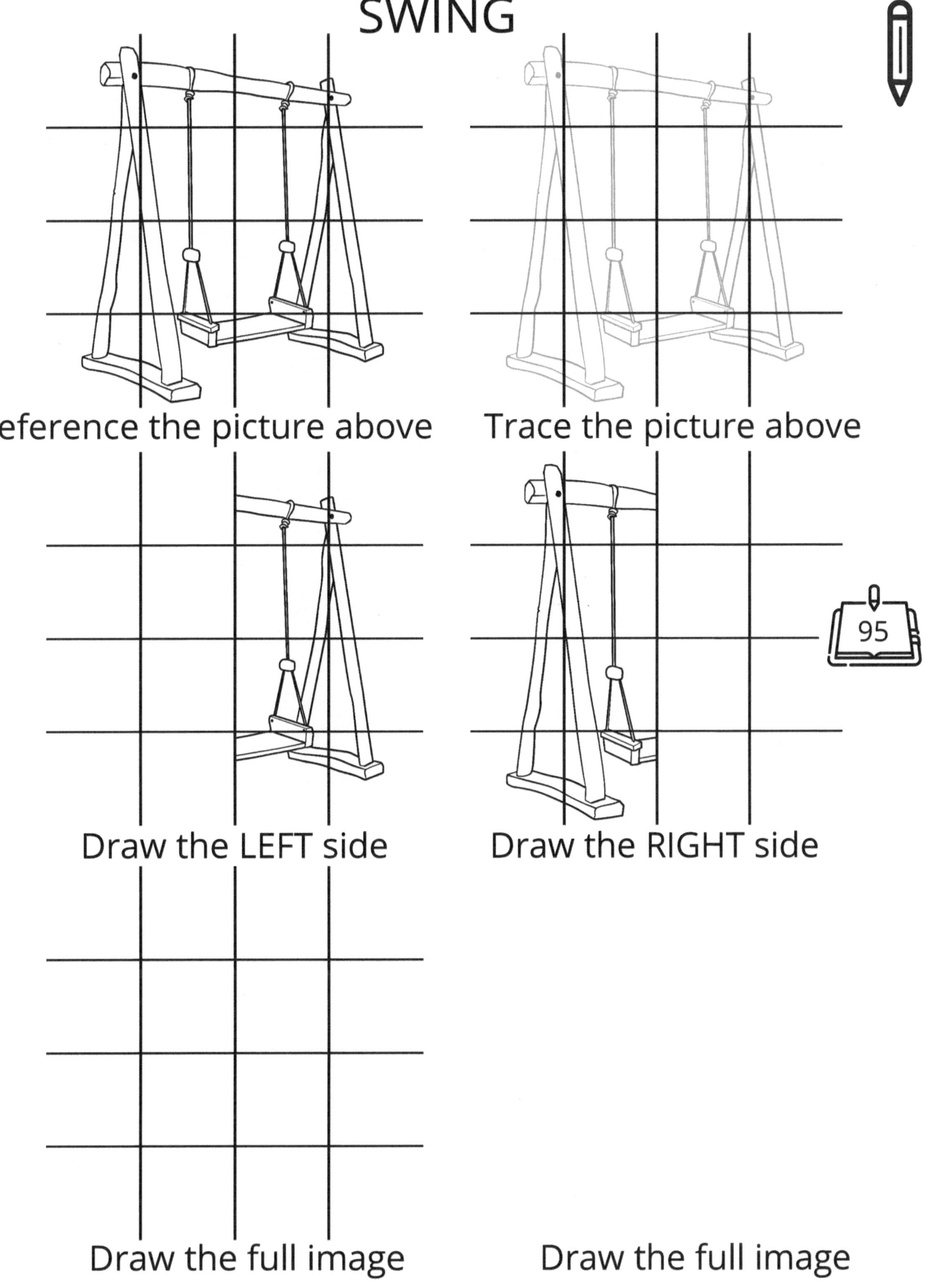

SOCCER BALL

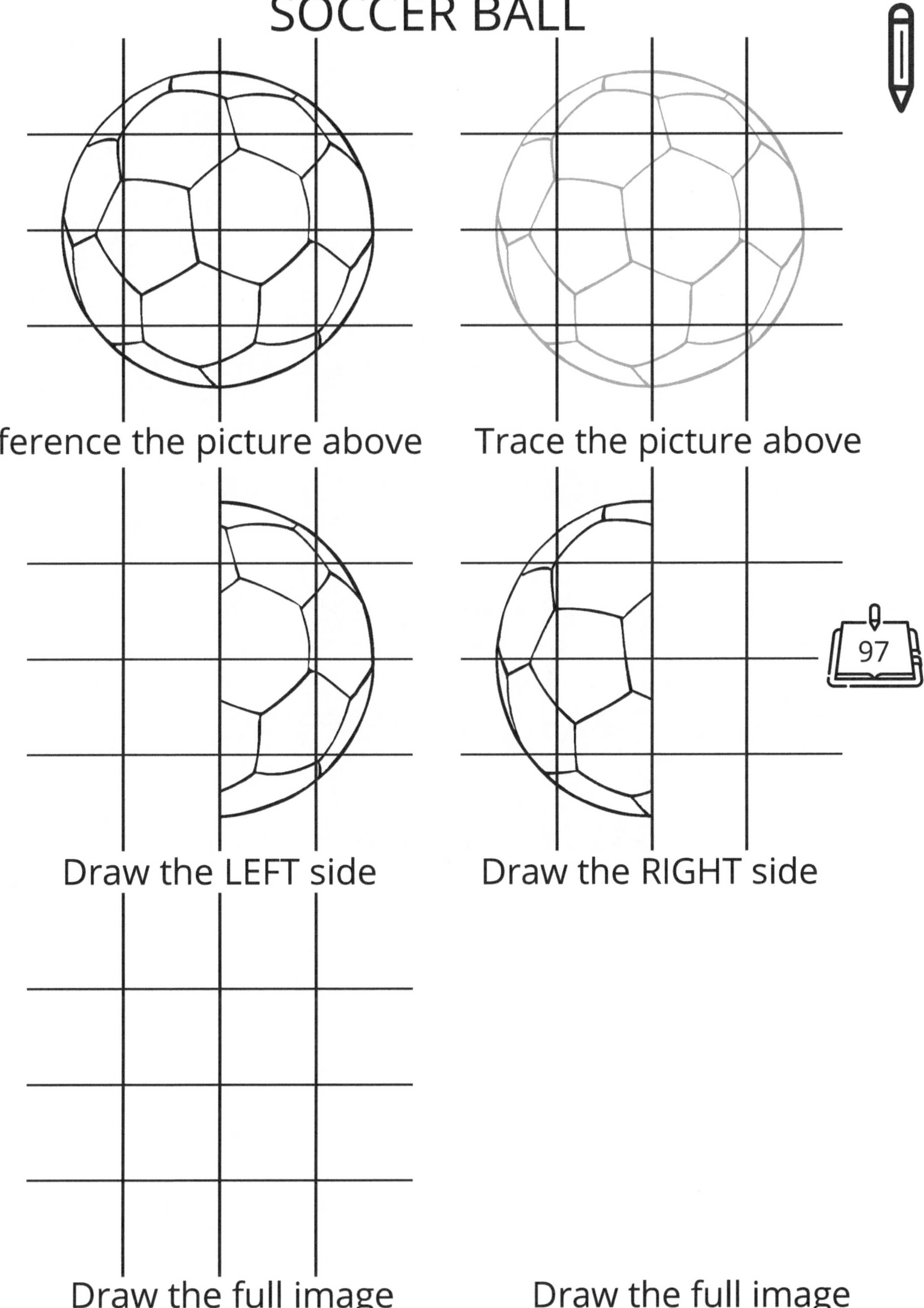

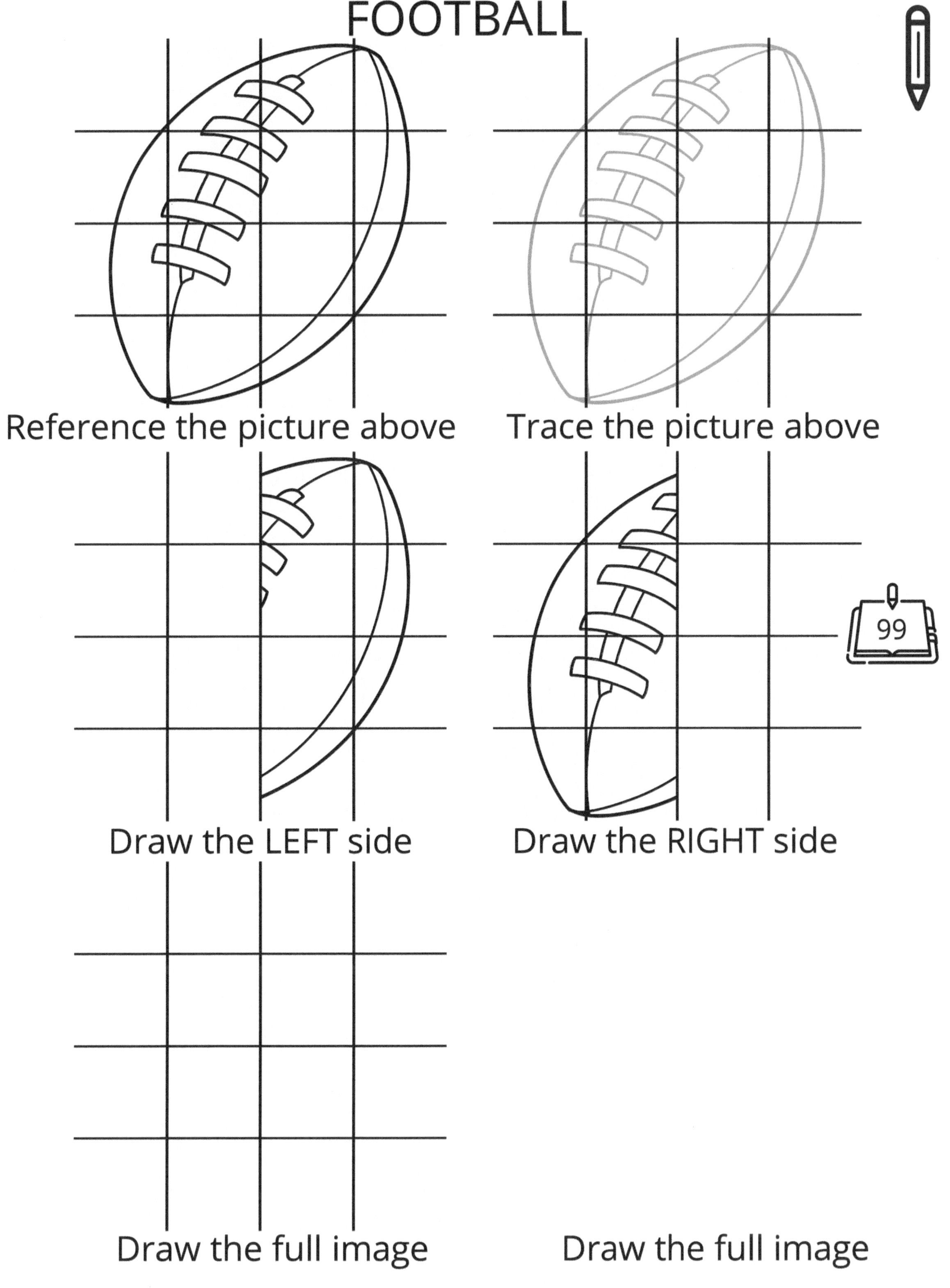
FOOTBALL
Reference the picture above
Trace the picture above
Draw the LEFT side
Draw the RIGHT side
Draw the full image
Draw the full image

HOCKEY

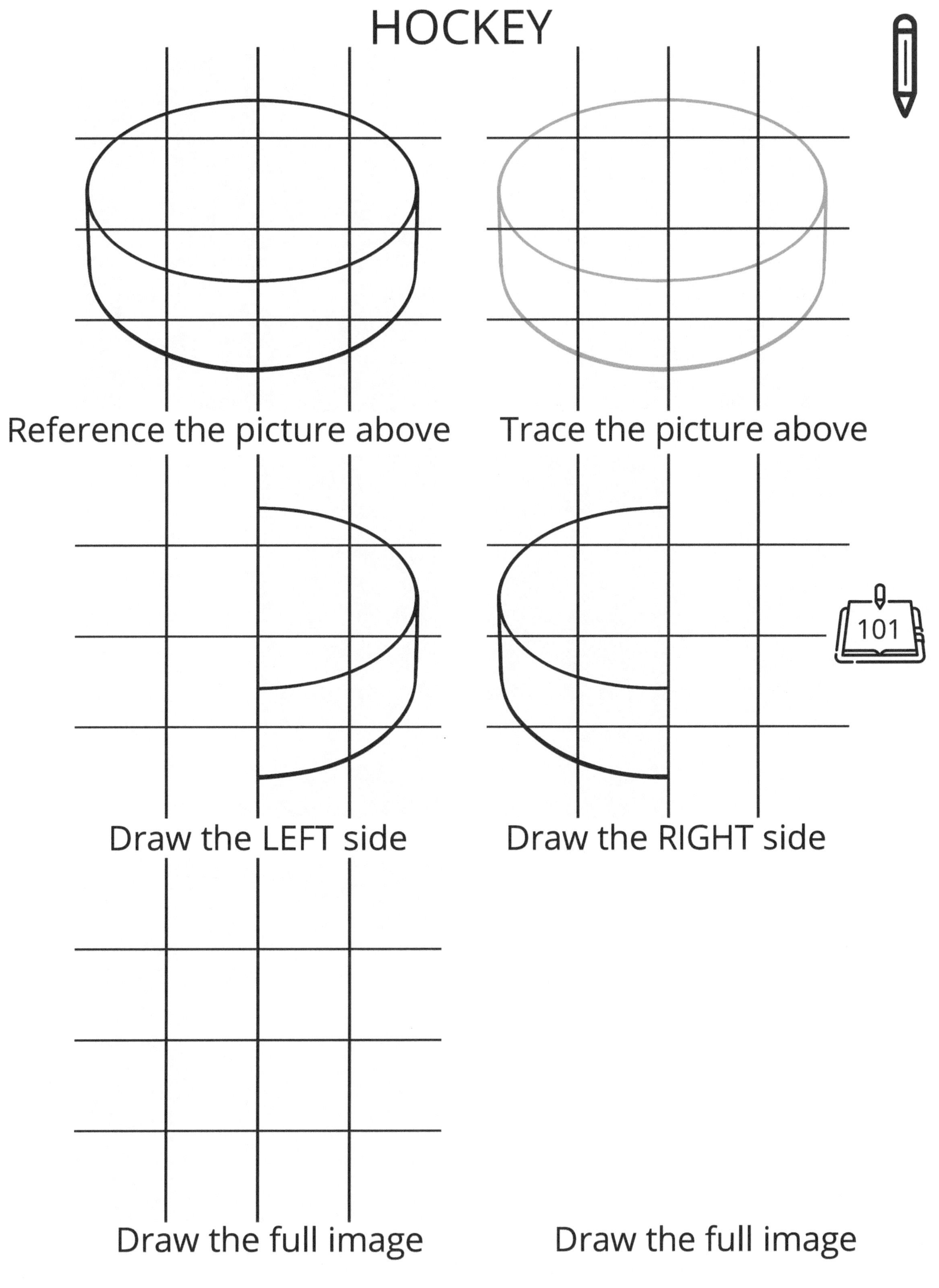

BASEBALL

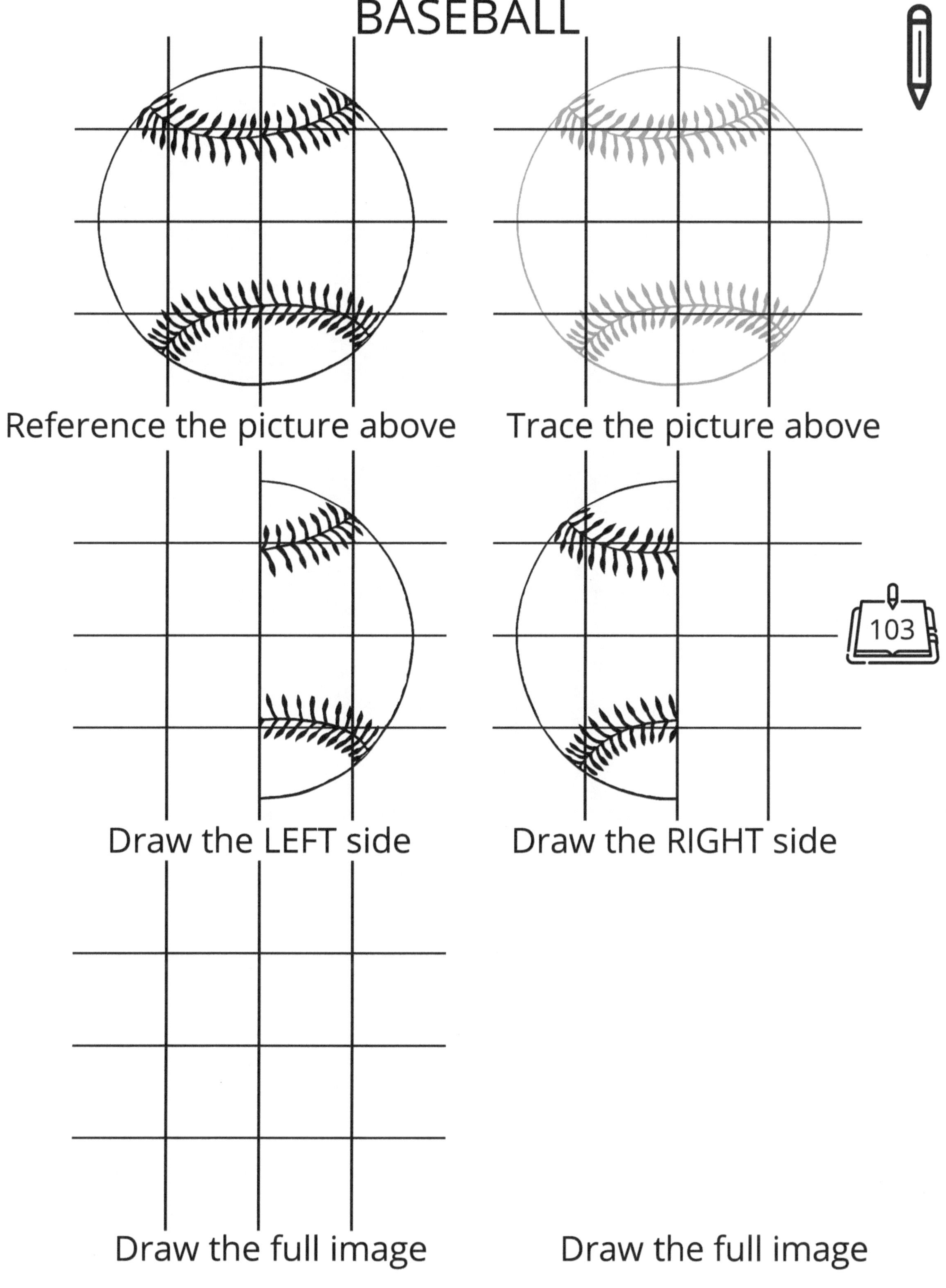

POGO STICK

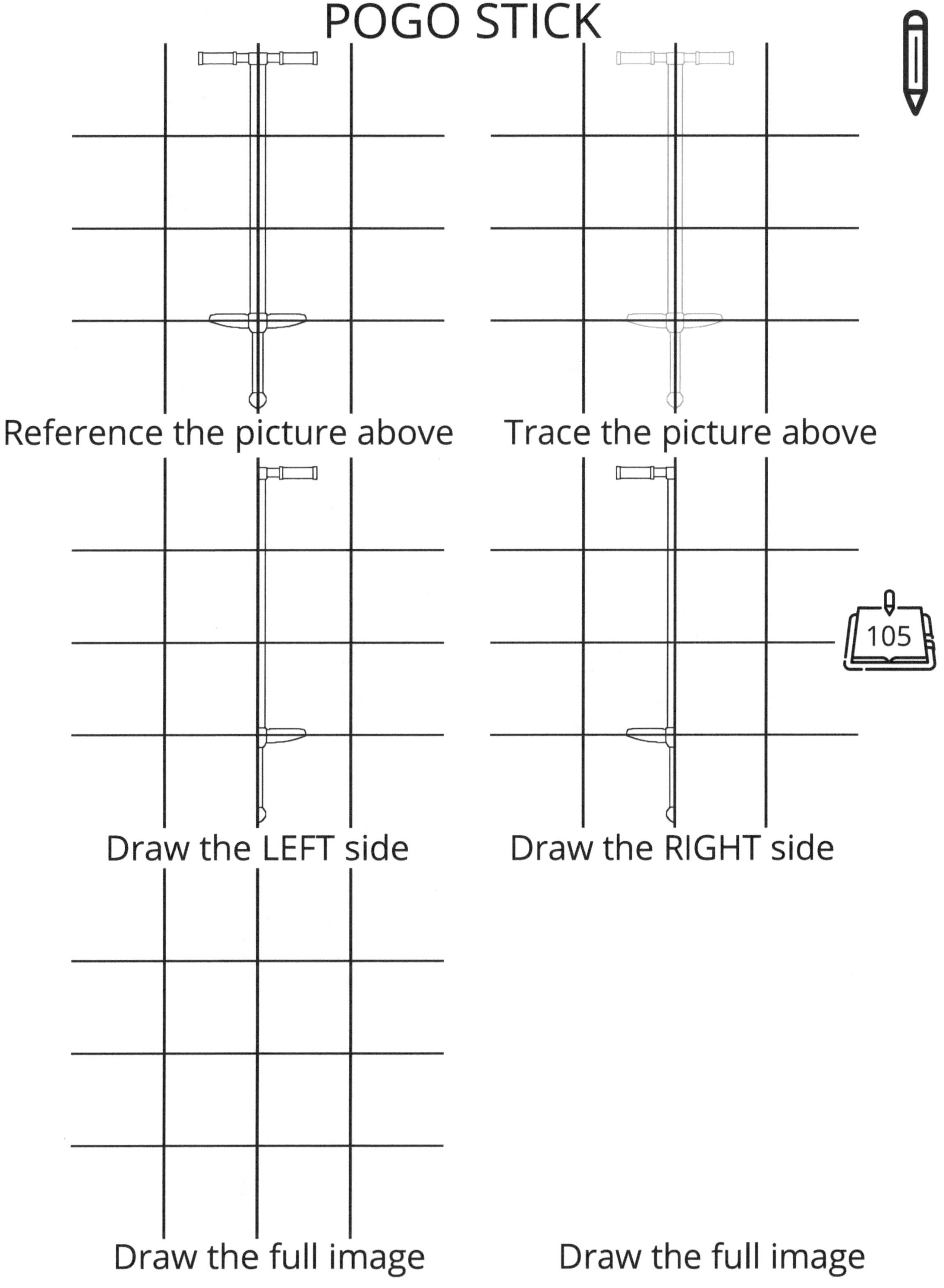

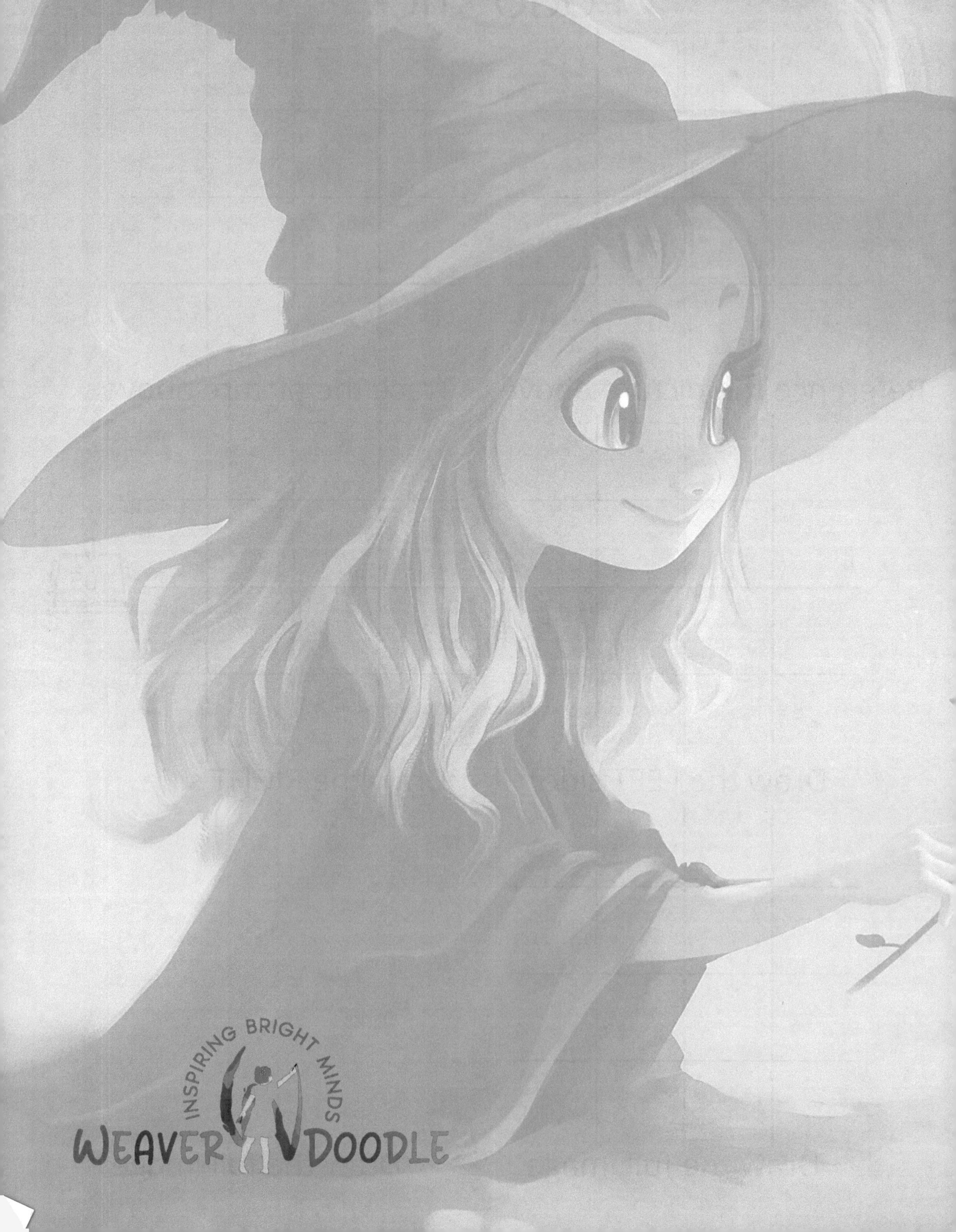

INSPIRING BRIGHT MINDS
WEAVER DOODLE

THANK YOU

Thanks again for supporting our small business. Your purchase of this book means everything to us.

PLEASE

If you haven't already, please take a moment to share your magical experience with a review on Amazon. Just follow the camera link below.

Made in United States
Troutdale, OR
01/12/2025

27878981R00060